PIONEERS
OF
COMPUTING

PIONEERS
OF
COMPUTING

F. Gareth Ashurst

FREDERICK MULLER LIMITED
LONDON

First published in Great Britain in 1983 by
Frederick Muller Limited, London SW19 7JZ

British Library Cataloguing In Publication Data

Ashurst, F. Gareth
    Pioneers of computing.
    1. Computers—Biography
    I. Title
    621.3819'5'0912   QA76

    ISBN 0–584–11009–X

Printed in Great Britain by
Redwood Burn Ltd, Trowbridge, Wiltshire.

Contents

To Helena, Justin and Julian,
for the future is theirs.

Acknowledgements

THE WRITING OF THIS BOOK would have been impossible without
access to many sources. All the books mentioned in the section on further reading have been consulted in some way.
Most extensive use has been made of the two works by Herman H Goldstine, the marvellous source book edited by Brian
Randell, and the very up-to-date collection edited by N.
Metropolis, J. Howlett and Gian-Carlo Rota, which contains
articles by Mauchly, Eckert and Zuse. I have also consulted
numerous other books, journals, newspapers and computer
manufacturers' literature to a lesser extent. It would be im-
practical, because of their nature and the number involved to
give a detailed acknowledgement of each of these, but their
help in preparing this book was most gratefully received.
However, all the inaccuracies, whether of fact or interpretation, in this book are mine and mine alone.

I would like to express my special thanks to my wife and
family who have shown untiring patience with me during the
various phases of the preparation of the book. Also my thanks
to my wife for her unfailing and readily volunteered hard
work in the typing of the manuscript.

Introduction

IN THIS PRESENT CENTURY we have witnessed the discovery, development and construction of many remarkable things. The invention of radio, the development of the aeroplane, the discovery of antibiotics and the preparation of plastics and synthetic polymers have each had revolutionary effects on our society. Our health, ability to travel, clothes, cars, houses and general prosperity have all increased enormously. Our whole lives have changed so much that we would scarcely recognise the everyday circumstances of people similar to us even just twenty years ago. Many of the pioneering events, such as the first flights by the Wright brothers, the discovery of penicillin by Fleming and the development of nylon by Carothers were accomplished almost singlehandedly, or perhaps, as with Fleming and Carothers, with one man leading a small team of expert helpers. Such enormous breakthroughs will rarely happen like this again. Arguably, the greatest achievement of the twentieth century, the landing of a man on the moon, was accomplished only with the aid of vast teams of men, hundreds of earlier discoveries, an incredible amount of money, and one very important machine. The machine was the computer, or to give it its full name, the digital electronic computer.

The computer has come to be a tool in all spheres of life, and to influence nearly every major scientific discovery and engineering advance in our society. It is inconceivable that any advance on the scale of those of the Wright brothers, or Fleming or Carothers would be made without a major role being played by the computer. Even changes in the social structure of our society, and the behaviour of people around us are strongly influenced by these machines. When we receive electricity bills, bank statements, watch television, go on a railway or air journey we are shadowed by the action of a computer. In commerce, government, navigation, science and engineering computers are at work on a very large scale. In shops, schools and even some of our homes computers are handled by quite ordinary people every day. The age of the computer has come; not always in the way it might have been envisaged by the pioneers, but it does influence our lives in a very marked way.

While it is easy to list creative achievements of men during this century, it is just as easy to recount their destructive phases. Strangely, out of the desire humans seem to have to destroy their fellow men have come many creations of mammoth proportions. So many things which have single important military applications turn out to have influenced multifarious peacetime applications. Indeed, they frequently are an aid to the regeneration and development of humanity. This was certainly the case with the modern electronic digital computer. It was the focusing effect of the Second World War which brought together the need for such a machine when already the technology for its development was available.

However, the history of the computer goes back many centuries before the nineteen thirties and forties. It is first important that we know clearly what we mean by a computer and computation. From before the beginning of recorded history, people have needed to count and to measure. Trading, following the calendar and navigation have all required the ability to count. Words like 'digit' and 'calculate' were derived from the names of common objects. Originally, counting must have been done with the fingers. Fingers and pebbles were perhaps just aids, but even the first real calculating device can be traced to at least the fourth century B.C. and it very probably dates from many centuries earlier.

The abacus, which was the name given to this by the Romans, was first used as a counting board divided into columns. In the columns, stones acted as counters which took certain values. These stones, or 'calculus' gave us the word 'calculate'. The abacus is a digital device since it relies on counting, rather than measuring, and digits (fingers) are used for this. This first digital computer has survived the test of time and in its form as a rack of beads it is often found as a child's toy or in primary school classrooms. As a means of calculating the abacus would not have survived thousands of years if had not been very effective. Once the technique of using this calculator has been learned it can be a remarkable aid to addition and subtraction. So much so, that abaci were a common object in the offices of oriental accountants, and as late as the nineteen sixties they were frequently found on the counters of shops in Peking.

Most modern computers are digital in operation because they solve their problems or process data by extremely rapid counting. There is, however, another type of calculating device; this uses the analogue principle. It is possible either with lengths of wood, mechanical systems or electric current to form a model or analogue of a problem. Then, by making measurements on the analogue it is possible to determine the solution of the problem. The essential feature of this form of computation is measurement, rather than counting. The simplest form of analogue computation probably takes place in maps and plans, with the ruler an important tool in the process. The first real computing device of this type however, was the slide rule which will be discussed in the next chapter.

Modern analogue computers are normally electrical and tend to be used for special purposes. Some are used to solve differential equations which often arise in intractable forms in engineering design, frequently in that of aeroplanes. It is a difficult and time-consuming task to connect these computers into the form which models a particular equation, and they are generally preferred over digital computers only in certain difficult circumstances. Analogue computers are also used as special purpose simulators. The control system of an aeroplane or a ship is frequently modelled on one of these machines to discover its gross behaviour under different sets of conditions. Also simulators for the training of aeroplane pilots are often machines of this kind.

Before a problem can be solved to the extent of having numerical answers it must be described mathematically. This is the work of one, or more often, a team of mathematicians and it demands a great deal of knowledge and insight into the overall problem.

The most direct knowledge available to the mathematician

is not always suitable for the arithmetic solution of a problem by a human or electronic computer. Napier changed multiplication into addition with his logarithms to make the solution of complex astronomical problems much easier. Since there are some operations and techniques used in mathematics, particularly those of calculus, that are not within the compass of an electronic computer, they must be transformed into the $+$, $-$, $\times$, $\div$ operations of arithmetic. The branch of mathematics which deals with this is called numerical analysis. Numerical analysis has a long history involving many of the famous mathematicians of the past beginning with Napier's logarithms; and it has progressed immensely with the advent of the electronic computer. Even so, it is based on an approximation to the solution of a mathematical problem and, while the approximation can often be made as close to the true solution as the mathematician pleases, it does not normally give the exact answer. The numerical analyst transforms the applied mathematician's work into mathematics which the computer can handle.

Many digital computers are not concerned with the solution of problems which have a large mathematical content; they deal mainly with data handling applications. Among these are rate demands, electricity bills, the control of the stock of a chain of stores, and the catalogue of a library. Even when little or no mathematics is involved, programs are still involved. There are many different types of programs (collectively known as software), all of which tell the hardware (the machinery of the computer), precisely what to do at some level in the process of computation or data handling. Programs are the instructions to the computer. Programmers construct these with absolute accuracy; this time-consuming and frequently frustrating process (especially when mistakes are made), is necessary because the hardware is not endowed with common sense. The machine does exactly what it is told, not what the programmer meant to tell it.

Hardware, software and numerical analysis have each been part of the development of the computer. Apart from the invention of logarithms, this book concentrates on the development of hardware, with some mention of the theoretical principles underlying its design and the theory of computation.

Even with the hardware there are considerable differences

in scale and complexity. The early pioneers, Pascal and Leibniz, developed machines which we would probably call calculators rather than computers. Indeed, although the calculator and the computer are now separate devices they have a common origin. It is with inventors like Charles Babbage that we first see the computer as being separate from the calculator and intended for a different purpose. When electricity was first applied in this field, it was to data processing with Hollerith rather than to engineering problem-solving as it was with Bush and his analogue computer. All the circumstances came together independently in at least two different places, and possibly a number of others, during the Second World War to advance electronic digital computers. However, these machines were very different from the ones which are now common throughout all aspects of commerce, industry, research and life generally.

The legacy of the pioneers described in this book is a long chain of ideas and machines, but frequently the men involved are more remarkable than anything they described or created. Thus, one of the most wonderful inventions of the twentieth century has only come about through the astounding insights and abilities of many fascinating people.

John Napier. (Photo: *Science Museum, London.*)

CHAPTER ONE

John Napier

MACHINES ARE NOW commonplace in the handling of numbers. Computers and calculators are used extensively in science, commerce and navigation. What was once done without the aid of mechanical or electronic gadgets was done by hand, or by brain. However, there are difficult and easy ways to do most things, and any method which makes a task easier than it would otherwise have been is to be valued. All things are equally easy when they are reduced to key strokes on a type-writer or calculator, but when we have to perform operations with our brains, some tasks are longer and more tedious than others. In arithmetic, addition is usually found to be easy while long division is fairly difficult. Multiplication is neither easy nor very hard if one knows the tables, but problems are often long and tedious.

As a simple example of this, imagine

$$\begin{array}{r} 423 \\ +\underline{276} \\ 699 \end{array}$$ where three separate additions are required

Now look at

$$\begin{array}{r} 423 \\ \times\ \underline{276} \\ 84,600 \\ 29610 \\ \underline{2538} \\ 116,748 \end{array}$$

we see that nine multiplications are required together with five main additions and a few carry over additions.

Although neither of these examples contains a prohibitive amount of work the multiplication requires about five times as much mental effort as the addition. Suppose now we compare

$$\begin{array}{r} 0{\cdot}5646424734 \\ +0{\cdot}6442176872 \\ \hline {}_{1\ 1}\qquad {}_{1\ 1} \\ 1{\cdot}2088601606 \end{array} \quad \text{with} \quad \begin{array}{r} 0{\cdot}5646424734 \\ \times 0{\cdot}6442176872 \\ \hline \end{array}$$

10 additions and carry overs

100 multiplications + 20 additions and carry overs

We do not often carry out calculations like these, and even the most opulent of electronic calculators will not give a twenty digit read out (answer).

During the sixteenth century, astronomers carried out long calculations in trigonometry, and examples like the last two were not uncommon. Extensive tables of sines were compiled during the 1500s and these were used by astronomers in the surveying of the heavens. It is important to point out that sines were not then described in quite the same ways as they are now, using a right-angled triangle

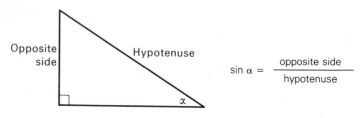

$$\sin \alpha = \frac{\text{opposite side}}{\text{hypotenuse}}$$

Although the word sine was introduced into Europe in about 1150 through a mistranslation by Robert of Chester of a word in an Arabic work on trigonometry, the trigonometric function was still recognised, as it had been for centuries, as the length of half the chord of a circle.

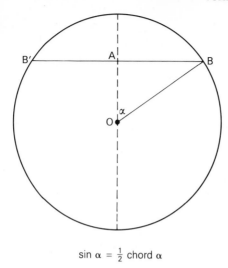

$$\sin \alpha = \tfrac{1}{2} \text{ chord } \alpha$$

The chord function was not usually expressed as a ratio and its value depended on the radius of the circle.

Any method to reduce the number of operations needed for multiplication has obvious advantages for the astronomer. It was also of advantage to the navigator and, to a lesser extent, the merchant. To reduce multiplication to a level of difficulty comparable with that of an addition with a similar number of digits would be a boon to these people. That such a method was found and was used extensively and almost exclusively as a method of performing long multiplication and division, the calculation of powers and roots, and combinations of any of these was one of the great achievements of man. The discovery of logarithms and their use, which was the new method, was instrumental in the subsequent growth in scientific knowledge of the heavens and eventually in most of the science and engineering we know now. It was only with the advent of the electronic calculator, that logarithms began to play subsidiary and less direct roles in science, although they are still of importance in advanced mathematics.

It is probably true that ideas are, and will always be, more important than machines. Logarithms are universally applicable to arithmetic problems, other than those involving addition and subtraction; and so a purely mental method has had a profound effect on the ways of the world.

The simple arithmetic sequence of positive integers had often been compared with the general geometric sequence of numbers with successive natural number exponents (powers)

$$0 \quad , \quad 1 \quad , \quad 2 \quad , \quad 3 \quad , \quad 4 \quad , \quad \ldots$$
$$x^0, \quad x^1, \quad x^2, \quad x^3, \quad x^4, \quad \ldots$$

and rules such as $x^2 \times x^3 = x^{2+3} = x^5$ and $x^4 \div x^2 = x^{4-2} = x^2$ were well known, but to put these ideas together in a useful calculating system was a monumental achievement. Perhaps it is all the more remarkable since the theory of logarithmic calculation was discovered so long ago, and was brought up to its present standard of usefulness by very few people. The first person to publish a work on logarithms was John Napier, Baron of Murchiston, in 1614.

John **Napier** was born at Murchiston Castle near Edinburgh in 1550. His father, Archibald Napier, was then a youth of sixteen. Much of the life of John is clouded by the mists of time. The life of even such a scientist, mathematician and man of rank from a noble family as was John Napier is not well chronicled. It is believed that he received his early education at home, but later he may have attended the High School at Edinburgh, which had existed since 1519. When he was about eleven years old he is thought to have spent some time in France. There is no doubt that as the first son of a noble Scottish family he would receive such benefits of education, travel and comfort as could be mustered in the sixteenth century.

Wherever he received his education, he was judged sufficiently schooled to enter the University of St. Andrews, the oldest of the Scottish universities, in 1563. He was then thirteen years old, which was the recognised age at which to begin university studies. The university was composed of three colleges. John entered St. Salvator's and boarded with its Head, Dr. John Rutherford. This cannot have been an altogether pleasant experience, for while we know little of Napier's pursuits at St. Salvator's, Rutherford's irascible and vitriolic nature was such that he has been mentioned in many writings. Rutherford was a leading scholar of the time, but, even as master of a college, he was not excused a public rebuke by the university authorities for his persistent violent temper and general inability to get along with his colleagues. How long the adolescent Napier stayed in the home of this man and studied at St. Andrews is not known, for he did not take a degree. Some time before 1566 he departed to carry on his studies at universities in other parts of Europe. There is no doubt that Napier was a very wise man, and no doubt that he was an able and demanding student. During the years after he left St. Salvator's he probably travelled from one university to another gathering all the knowledge which he could from their professors; this was the tradition of the time for those with real intellectual ability and the wherewithal to travel.

By 1571 Napier had returned to his native Scotland. Not this time to Murchiston Castle, but to Gartness in Stirlingshire, where his father owned land. John was to manage this estate until the elder man died in 1608. As laird of this area, John had considerable power, influence and responsibilities. His workers depended on him for support and protection, and in those times when might was as important as right, rough justice (and sometimes injustice) was the stock in trade of the proud and derermined Scots.

In 1572 he married Elizabeth Stirling, the daughter of Sir James Stirling, the owner of the estate which adjoined his. The marriage was blessed with a son and a daughter, but his wife did not live to enjoy many more years, for John Napier was married a second time in 1579.

The Napier family was renowned for its abilities. In the past, its members had risen to high ranks as soldiers, envoys and statesman. Three Napiers had been Provosts of Edinburgh, the family were hereditary poulterers to the king and John's father was to achieve high office as Master of the Mint. If there could be any distinction between such clever and trusted men, it was to the benefit of John. He was recognised as the family adviser because of his skill in debate, his understanding of people and his knowledge of the law. There is little doubt that he was sought out by others because of his cleverness and that he performed official missions important to Scotland. John, like his father, was a determined Protestant. In the religious troubles of the times, when Catholic and Protestant were locked in battle and the religious and regal future of Scotland were the spoils of war, John Napier never wavered. As we will see, he devoted much of his time to theology, and his view of the Church of Rome will be mentioned later.

For a man so deeply involved with Christian thought in such a direct and positive way, the view in which he was held by the people around him, and even those further afield in other parts of Scotland, might at first seem strange, John Napier was thought to practice witchcraft. Although witchcraft was not uncommon in Scotland during these times, and indeed Napier probably had the opportunity to join one of the covens of witches that then existed, it seems strange that a man of such polarised Christian beliefs should become involved. It is much more likely that the sparkling manifestations of his practical wisdom would dazzle the minds of the unschooled peasants, and thus be attributed to supernatural powers.

One particular story about Napier which smacks of witchcraft, but really involves nothing of the kind, concerns his supposed familiar, a jet-black cockerel. At this time some of his valuable personal possessions went missing. As he believed that one or more of his servants was involved he devised a secret and cunning plan. His cockerel was first placed in a dark room, then he let it be known that when the thief's hands touched the cockerel's neck, the creature would cry out. Each domestic was given instructions to enter the room and stroke the bird. Little did they know that their wise master had previously coated it with soot. During the whole proceedings there was no cry from the bird, but Napier quickly found one pair of clean and unblackened hands.

Another story of his magical powers also involves birds. Napier protested that his neighbour's pigeons were eating all his corn. The neighbour told him in a very unsubtle way not to bother him with such lies and that even if this was true he was not going to do anything about it. Napier replied that he would impound the birds and keep them as his own. The neighbour doubted him until he saw them the next morning littering Napier's fields and calmly being collected by the laird's servants, apparently neither wanting to nor being able to fly away. Was this magic or science?

Although Napier was recognised as an honourable and trustworthy man, either honour had a somewhat different meaning in the sixteenth century, or Napier had occasional lapses, or, which was more likely, guile, cunning and sometimes sharp practice were needed to stay alive and to prosper. There is obviously little doubt that Napier encouraged those around him to believe that he practiced witchcraft. Such a belief on the part of the peasants was to his advantage; however, it was not just peasants who were deluded. In one of his more dubious deeds, he entered into a contract with the rascally outlawed noble Robert Logan of Restalrig to locate a concealed treasure in Fast Castle. A strange contract was drawn up and signed by the two men. If Napier should succeed, he was to get one-third of the fortune and the contract was to be destroyed. Presumably he was sought for this task because of his supposed supernatural powers, as no one would give away so much money without first exhausting all the more practical methods. Since the contract still exists, it seems likely that Napier failed in this venture.

Even though he often had effective practical means at his disposal, Napier was no stranger to litigation. By this means he had varying degrees of success; however, he was a determined man, for he is known to have petitioned the Privy Council on more than one occasion.

In 1608, after the death of his father, John Napier returned to Murchiston Castle and succeeded to the title of Baron of Murchiston. The obligations of rank as well as the practicalities of managing lands must have conspired to fill his time, but, as we will see, he was now extremely active in his mathematical researches. As one of both noble birth and wisdom and living so close to Edinburgh, he was frequently involved with important matters concerning the city. Unfortunately, this busy period turned out to be much shorter than his stay in Stirlingshire. John Napier died nine years later at Murchiston Castle on the 4th April 1617. His death was attributed to gout, a condition he had suffered from for many years. He is believed to have been buried in the old St. Cuthbert's Church in Edinburgh.

Napier contributed to many fields of knowledge, almost all of them eminently practical. As farming was his livelihood, he investigated the growth of crops and the well-being of animals. He used the first fertilizer, other than dung. This was common salt. There was also a series of inventions for defence against invasion. One of them was a large parabolic mirror which could focus the rays of the sun on a ship two or more miles distant, and thus destroy it by burning. There were other mirrors with somewhat less devastating purposes. Napier devised an artillery piece which could sweep a whole field clear of the enemy. There was also a war chariot which could spread destruction on all sides by pouring molten metal. He also devised a ship for sailing under water. The seaworthiness of this submarine is, however, open to dispute.

Mention has already been made of Napier's religious studies; now he is considered to be an early and major Scottish theologian. His famous work in this area was the book *A Plaine Discovery of the Whole Revelation of St. John*. The 'Whole Revelation of St. John' or 'The Apocalypse of St. John' is another name for the Biblical 'Book of Revelations'. Napier's book was published in 1593 and it quickly became the sixteenth century equivalent of a bestseller. Five editions in English had been published by 1645; there were also three early editions in Dutch, four in German and no less than nine in French between 1602 and 1607. It was the result of many years of scholarly study and meditation and was a genuine attempt to interpret the Bible and show its relevance to human life. Napier was concerned with finding the answers to certain questions, the most important of which was the meaning of the 'Book of Revelations'. In the first part of *A Plaine Discovery* . . . there are thirty-six propositions or proposed answers to the questions, each followed by a justification. The rest of the book is a verse by verse commentary on the 'Book of Revelations'. His most interesting conclusions are that the Pope is the Antichrist and that the world will decline after 1541 and end at the latest by 1786. He also suggested that the Day of Judgement would occur between 1688 and 1700. These prognostications now seem very strange, and they are perhaps apt to be dismissed lightly by many people, even Biblical scholars, but for Napier this was a valid attempt to discover and interpret that which has not, even now, been satisfactorily explained. This book was to raise his esteem to an international level as a scholar and it was to have a major intellectual effect at the beginning of the seventeenth century. However, it was to have neither the effect nor the usefulness of his greatest research, the discovery of logarithms.

We saw earlier the comparison of simple arithmetic and geometric sequences. The properties of this comparison were first investigated by Michael Stifel of Jena in 1553. Whether or not Napier was familiar with Stifel's work is not known, but certainly ideas concerning these properties of numbers occupied his thoughts for many years. Napier, as has already been mentioned, was a very practical man, and he was prepared to devote his time to practical methods of calculation. The development of the theory of his logarithms could be carried out intermittently until he struck useful ideas, but the actual calculation of tables required determined effort, with considerable belief in their usefulness and applicability, since possibly thousands of hours were spent on their calculation. Napier's first publication concerning logarithms was a book with an awesome Latin title, which is now usually shortened to the *Descriptio*. This work was published in 1614 and was the first set of logarithm tables ever published. It represented at least twenty years work in calculating the tables and possibly much longer in the development of the ideas of logarithms. In the *Descriptio* he explained the nature of logarithms and their properties and how to use the tables, but not how they were calculated. From his writings, it seems that, like many fathers of great inventions, he was a little unsure as to how the world would receive his child. His creation was fully explained in another book, the *Constructio* (another contraction of a long Latin title) which was published posthumously by his own son Robert in 1619, although it had been written several years earlier.

The word logarithm was devised by Napier from two Greek words which together mean 'ratio number'. Originally he had given the name 'artificiales' to his new numbers. At the beginning of his *Constructio* Napier writes: 'A Logarithmic Table is a small table by the use of which we can obtain a knowledge of all geometrical dimensions and motions in space, by a very easy calculation'. A little further on in the work he gives his precise definition of the logarithm: 'The logarithm of a given sine is that number which has increased arithmetically with the same velocity throughout as that which the radius began to decrease geometrically, and in the same time as radius has decreased to the given sine'.

Napier saw the whole process as a correspondence between

the simultaneous motions of two points; one increasing uniformly, the other decreasing in velocity in such a way that the greater distance it reached from its starting point the slower it became, with its speed proportional to the distance it still had to go along its path. The path the points travelled over was the length of the whole sine, or the radius of the circle whose semichords were used as sines; in Napier's table this distance, r, was 10^7.

Uniform increase

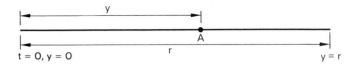

Decrease in proportion to x

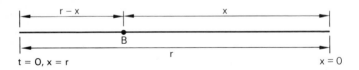

In mathematical symbols, Napier's Logarithm $x = r \log_e \frac{r}{x}$ or, particularly Nap $\log = 10^7 \log_e \frac{10^7}{x}$, where e is the exponential number $2 \cdot 71829 \ldots$ Note that these logarithms are neither the ones which we find in our books of tables nor are they the ones commonly described as 'Naperian Logarithms', which were actually devised by Kepler.

For those readers interested in the mathematics of this definition the following derivation may be of use.

In Figure 1 $\frac{dy}{dt} = r$, and in Figure 2 $\frac{d}{dt}(r - x) = x$

i.e. $y = rt + c$ $\qquad\qquad\qquad\qquad -\frac{dx}{dt} = x$

Now when t = o, y = o
i.e. c = o
Hence y = rt

i.e. $\log_e x + k = -t$
when t = o, x = r
i.e. $k = -\log_e r$

i.e. $\log_e \frac{x}{r} = -t$

Hence $x = re^{-t}$

Combining these two equations by eliminating t, gives $x = re^{-y/r}$. Taking logarithms to the base e of each side, gives:

$$\log_e x = \log_e r - \frac{1}{r} \log_e e^y$$

$$\text{i.e. } \log_e \frac{x}{r} = -\frac{1}{r} \log_e e^y$$

$$\text{Hence } y = r \log_e \frac{r}{x}$$

But y = Nap log x and $r = 10^7$

$$\therefore \text{ Nap log } x = 10^7 \log_e \frac{10^7}{x}$$

We are used to performing logarithmic calculations now by changing products directly into sums of logarithms and quotients directly into differences of logarithms, but this is generally not possible in Napier's logarithms since Nap log 10^7 = 0 not Nap log 1. So we get the rules,

Nap log xy = Nap log x + Nap log y − Nap log 1,

since Nap log xy = $10^7 \log_e \frac{10^7}{xy} = 10^7 \log_e \frac{10^7}{x} \cdot \frac{10^7}{y} \cdot \frac{1}{10^7}$

$= 10^7 \log_e \frac{10^7}{x} + 10^7 \log_e \frac{10^7}{y} - 10^7 \log_e 10^7$

and Nap log $\frac{x}{y}$ = Nap log x − Nap log y + Nap log 1.

The following examples illustrate the use of Napier's logarithms.

56 × 95	Nap log 56	120927440
	+ Nap log 95	115642188
		236569628
	− Nap log 1	161180957
5320		75388671

$56 \div 95$	Nap log 56	120927440
	− Nap log 95	115642188
		5285252
	+ Nap log 1	161180957
0·589473656 (to 9 significant figures)		166466209

In the fifty or so pages of explanation, which accompanied the ninety pages of tables in the *Descriptio* was a discussion of the solution of triangles. It was here that Napier gave his formulae for the solution of right-angled spherical triangles.

The famous Napier's Bones or Rods were described in his *Rabdologia*, a book published in 1617, the year of his death. A set of Napier's Bones is a device for multiplication. It consists of ten strips or rods, each with the multiplication table for a number between one and ten.

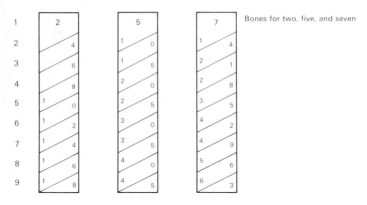

Bones for two, five, and seven

To multiply 257 by 4, place the bones together in the order 2, 5, 7, and read along the line opposite 4.

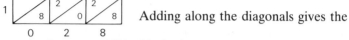 Adding along the diagonals gives the

required answer 1028. Similarly, multiplication by forty is effected by adjoining a zero, i.e. 10280 and multiplication by forty-four would be carried out by adding these two sub-totals i.e. 10280

      1028

    11308

By using combinations of the full ten rods, adjoining zeros

where necessary, and combining subtotals, a very effective method of multiplying was available for those not greatly skilled in this art. Napier's Bones have been used as a calculating device for centuries, and they can still be purchased as a teaching aid for use in schools. There is also a cylindrical form of the Bones in which ten rollers, each containing the full ten Bones set longitudinally, can be rotated to set up a long multiplication problem. As the cylinders are firmly located in a wooden box, the answer can be found fairly easily, even though some addition along diagonals may be necessary. Although there is some slight evidence that Napier may have devised this wooden calculating machine, it is general attributed to Gaspard Schott who described this device in 1668.

The *Rabdologia* also contains the first suggestion of the use of the full stop as a means of separating whole numbers from decimal fractions. This idea which is now commonly used, although it took quite a long time for its general adoption, is also mentioned in the *Constructio*. Napier did not, however, invent decimal fractions; these were the creation of Simon Stevin in 1585.

After their publication, Napier's logarithms came quickly to the attention of Henry **Briggs**, one of England's leading mathematicians. Briggs was born at Warley Wood near Halifax in February 1561. He attended a grammar school near Warley during his childhood. In 1577, at the age of sixteen, he went up to St. John's College, Cambridge. Eleven years later after a distinguished career as an undergraduate and graduate student, he was made a fellow of his college. Shortly afterwards he also took up teaching duties in Cambridge university. By 1596 his reputation was such that he was appointed as the first Professor of Geometry at Gresham College, and he held this position for twenty-three years. When, in 1619, Sir Henry Savile resigned the professorship of astronomy which he had founded at Oxford University, he asked Briggs to take over the position. Briggs held both professorships simultaneously for a year, until he resigned that at Gresham College. From then onwards he concentrated in his life around his work at Oxford. Briggs died at Merton College, where he had been elected a fellow on the 26th January 1630.

Although it is as a mathematician and, in particular, a developer of logarithms that he is principally remembered, he also contributed greatly to the theory of navigation. He was especially interested in the use of the earth's magnetic field as an aid to navigation, and in producing detailed navigational tables. He also published detailed procedures for following particular sea routes.

Briggs was no stranger to the compilation of tables. At least ten years before he became involved with logarithms, he had compiled a table of sines to fifteen places and one of tangents and secants to ten places. When he learned of Napier's work he was struck with the importance of the discovery and its usefulness in astronomy and navigation. In his lectures at Gresham College, logarithms became a topic of great interest to himself and his students. He played about with the ideas of his own and then he determined to meet Napier, the maestro. In 1615 he made the long, arduous journey from London to Edinburgh and stayed for about a month with Napier. When the two mathematicians met they were, according to at least one report, struck with such admiration for each other that about a quarter of an hour passed before a word was spoken. At Gresham College, Briggs had come to the conclusion that logarithms would be easier to use if the $\log 1 = 0$. When he advanced this idea to Napier, the Scotsman replied that it had already occurred to him, and that calculation would be made easier if also $\log 10 = 10^{10}$. This is by no means as strange as it might seem when now $\log 10 = 1$; it merely indicates that whole numbers to ten figures would be used instead of decimal fractions. (The first decimal logarithms produced were those for sines and tangents. They were compiled by Edmund Gunter.)

On returning to London, Briggs set about calculating these new and improved logarithms. The following year he visited Napier again and showed him his work so far and discussed improvements to the complicated task of calculating the new logarithms. In 1617, after Napier's death, Briggs published his first table, the *Logarithmorum Chilias Prima*, which was the first appearance of common, base ten, logarithms. This, like his more comprehensive *Arithmetica Logarithmica* of 1624, gave logarithms to fourteen places. Again these were really tables of logarithms of sines, but expressed simply as logarithms, Briggs $\log x = 10^9 \log_{10} x$. These logarithms allow calculations to be carried out in a way very similar to that of using the ordinary logarithms of the present.

The work of Napier and Briggs quickly caught the attention of the scientific community, and over the centuries there has been a succession of determined logarithm table compilers from Ursinus, Kepler and Vlacq and Wolfrom with his mammoth forty place exponential or natural logarithm tables to the more modern ones: Peano, Knott and Castle.

Although Napier is unanimously credited with the discovery of logarithms, he is not the only one with a claim to the invention. Joost **Burgi**, a Swiss watch and instrument maker published a table of anti-logarithms in 1620. Remember, an anti-logarithm table is just a logarithm table turned inside out (with the body of the table made up of the numbers around the outside of a logarithm table and the outside made up from the innards of a logarithm table) and so it is not really a different thing. Burgi was born in 1552 in St. Gall. His work was so good that he gained commissions from the courts of Prague and Kassel. He also made astronomical clocks and carried out astronomical observations. Like many astronomers he was interested in trigonometry and was concerned with the use of tables. He was known to the great astronomer Kepler and is believed to have acquainted him with his researches on logarithms. Certainly, Kepler was involved in developing logarithms, but he is also known to have used Napier's tables. Burgi's logarithms are to the curious base of $(1{\cdot}0001)^{\frac{1}{10}}$. They were very inconvenient to use and generally inferior to those of Napier, even though they were printed using two different colours to guide the mathematician. Although Burgi's tables were published after Napier's it is known that he had been at work on them for many years. But so had Napier. Whereas it is not possible to say whether the notion of logarithms came first into the mind of Napier or that of Burgi, it is certainly true that Napier's was the better system, and it is from his system that the development of logarithms has progressed.

A logarithm table is a device for numerical analysis, not a calculator or computer. However, it was not long before analogue calculators were invented that used scales derived from a table of logarithms. In 1620 Edmund Gunter, who succeeded Briggs as Professor of Astronomy at Gresham College, produced a two foot line of logarithms which was etched onto a wooden rule. The 'Gunter's Scale' was frequently used for complex calculations; and it was still in use with mariners at the beginning of the nineteenth century. Dividers were used so that multiplication and division could be performed by the addition and subtraction of lengths of Gunter's line. Gunter was a friend and, for one year, a colleague of Briggs, and no doubt was given help, and advice by him. Also like Briggs he was involved with the earth's magnetic field and the angle of declination. Gunter was born in Hertfordshire in 1581 and died at Gresham College on the 10th December 1626.

Another contemporary and friend of both Briggs and Gunter was William Oughtred. Oughtred was born at Eton on the 5th March 1571. After studying at Cambridge he took a living as a clergyman at Albury near Guildford, where he eventually died on the 30th June 1660. Oughtred was one of the leading mathematicians of the time, but for our purposes he is remembered because in 1621, he used two Gunter scales sliding over each other to perform calculations without the need of dividers. In his book, *Circles of Proportion* which is really a treatise on navigation, he described trigonometrical scales and Gunter's scales in a circle. So he also had a hand in the circular slide rule. It was, however, left to Richard Delamain to give the first full description of the circular and cylindrical slide rules in 1630.

The last step in the invention of the straight slide rule as we know it was when Robert Bissaker, in 1654, constructed a rule made from a fixed stock with a sliding tongue, a Gunter's scale being fixed on both the stock and the tongue.

The slide rule was an extremely useful calculating device. It was a simple, practical analogue device which was small and, with fair use, indestructible. Like the logarithms it embodies, it has had the longest history of all, other than the abacus. In only a few years, the slide rule has disappeared from being the constant companion of the engineer and scientists, and it has been replaced by the electronic calculator. It now seems very unlikely that it will ever again become anything else but the museum piece it is already. However, logarithms will always have a place. They are interesting and have useful connections with several branches of mathematics, such as integration, in a role which is not directly related to calculation. Also they are the basis of the calculations performed by electronic calculators. But logarithm tables as little grey, brown or blue books have already vanished from laboratories and drawing offices, and only linger in classrooms because of the affection teachers have for them. They are under sentence of retirement and soon they will be pensioned off to reside in cupboards for a number of years before being consigned to the rubbish heap.

Blaise Pascal. (Photo: *Science Museum, London.*)

CHAPTER TWO

Blaise Pascal

SO FAR as we know, the first mechanical calculating machine other than possibly those based on the principle of Napier's Bones was built in 1623. This was the invention of Wilhelm **Schickard**. Schickard was born in 1592 and died in 1635. He lived during the turbulent times of the Thirty Years War. Schickard rose to become professor of mathematics, astronomy and Hebrew at the University of Tubingen. His machine is known from the discovery of two of his letters in the papers of the astronomer Johannes Kepler, who discovered the nature of the motion of the planets. The letters, one of 1623 and the other of 1624, said that the calculator added, subtracted, divided and multiplied. It was also described as being able to carry tens and hundreds, and it generally carried out the operations in an automatic fashion. The second letter says that Schickard ordered a machine to be built for Kepler by a local instrument maker but that the machine and drawings were destroyed in a fire at the man's workshop. Since the discovery of the existence of his calculating machine in 1957, a number of working models have been made from the information contained in the letters by Professor Bruno Baron von Freytag-Loringhoff and his highly skilled assistants.

The first extant calculating machine was the creation of a much more famous personage. Whenever one reads of Blaise **Pascal** it is rarely that his calculating machine comes near the beginning of a list of his achievements. Anyone of a number of his accomplishments would have guaranteed him fame. If one looks in a library or a bookshop one is likely to find his classic work of French literature, *Pensées* (Thoughts). Perhaps if one looks a little further one will discover his strong connection with theology and the Catholic faith. These are the aspects of his endeavours which are most often mentioned but to mathematicians he was an exponent of their art. As a physicist, he proved the existence of a vacuum and made some important discoveries about atmospheric pressure which we take for granted today. For the physician he invented the syringe and for the engineer he invented the hydraulic press. He devised a system of public transport by horse-drawn omnibuses which began operation in Paris in 1660, and for the gardener and builder he invented the wheelbarrow.

Blaise Pascal was born at Clermont in Auvergne on the 19th June 1623. His family were Catholics and the Catholic faith was to play an important part in much of his life. His father, Etienne, was a public official of high importance. He was then *Conseiller Elu pour le Roi* in the electorate of Bas-Auvergne at Clermont. The following year Etienne was appointed President of the Cour des Aides. He is also remembered in mathematics for his deep study of the 'limacon of Pascal'. This is in fact a family of curves with an equation of the form $r = a + b\cos\theta$ in polar co-ordinates. Its animate description (the snail of Pascal) was given by another famous mathematician of the time, Gilles Persone de Roberval.

Antoinette, Blaise's mother, came from a local family of well-to-do merchants and high ranking civil servants. Alas, she was soon to die, leaving Blaise, then an infant of three, and his two sisters Gilberte and Jacqueline. Even before this cruel event, life was unkind to Blaise. Shortly after a baby is born the three gaps in its cranium, the fontanelles, which facilitate its birth, begin to join with the rest of the skull. That this normal aspect of growth never properly occurred in his case was to be the probable cause of much of the ill health which he suffered throughout his life, and of a number of curious events. It is known that he suffered a terrible illness when he was one year old. Just as in the slightly earlier times of Napier, belief in witchcraft was strong and the state of the young Pascal was soon attributed to a witch's spell. Even a perpetrator of this vicious crime was found. Apparently an old woman had asked Etienne Pascal to defend her in a court action in which she claimed she had been unjustly accused. The elder Pascal having believed otherwise refused to act on her behalf. Her retribution on the lawyer had been the spell on his son. It is said that the old woman could not remove the malevolence but could transfer it to something else. After a number of experiments with unfortunate animals, a cat, no doubt short on its nine lives, saw the last of its days. Honour largely being satisfied all round, Blaise was left to recover as best he could.

Etienne Pascal was both a good and fortunate man. He was prepared to devote his life to the upbringing of his three children and he had the financial means with which to do it. After his wife's death, he sold his post to his brother in 1631 and moved the family to Paris. Etienne was also an enlightened man for his time and he devoted a lot of consideration to the education of his offspring. He allowed Blaise to develop his intense curiosity and learn about the things he encountered. At the same time, Etienne fostered his son's ability to reason and judge. This was all in stark contrast to the rote learning of the rules of Latin grammar which was largely the substance of the customary rigorous classical education. The young Pascal was soon carrying out scientific investigations into the nature of things around him. These early years contributed much to his comprehension of the scientific method which he was to use in his mature experiments, when many of his contemporaries were hamstrung by their unsuitable design of experiments. At the same time Blaise was encouraged to study the Bible and the history and doctrines of the Church. Etienne's plan for his son's education embraced the maxim that the child should always be superior to his work. As his curriculum was to unfold, Blaise was to study general knowledge up to twelve years of age, Latin, Greek, history and geography from then until sixteen, when he was to admit geometry to his studies.

The fact that Blaise's father was an accomplished mathematician and that the boy himself was incurably curious, caused the carefully designed curriculum to go astray. Although Blaise was protected from the study of geometry, which was largely the composition of mathematics at that time, he gathered enough from his mentor to begin it on his own. When he was about twelve, his father found him deep in his geometrical studies. In his ignorance of their names, he had called straight lines 'bars' and circles 'rounds'. One story relates how he discovered the early propositions of Euclid, even in the same order of their occurrence in that work. However, it does appear that he proved that the sum of the angles of a triangle is two right angles by his own efforts.

That the elder Pascal was a man of considerable intellect is obvious, and it is equally obvious that such a person should search out and be sought by other intellectuals. Throughout his time in Paris he was a member of the then uninstituted gathering of the *Academie Mersenne* which included the mathematicians Mersenne, Desargues and Roberval as well as a number of other distinguished thinkers. This gathering was later to become the *Academie Libre* and finally the *Academie des Sciences*. As Blaise's intellect developed he was also encouraged by his father and the other members to attend the meetings and through them he became attracted to the work of Desargues and what is now termed projective geometry. When he was sixteen Blaise wrote a short paper (it was only one page) on the geometry of his mentor which contained a new and rather startling result. It contained what is now called 'Pascal's theorem' which says: If a hexagon is inscribed in a conic (circle, ellipse, parabola or hyperbola), then the three points of intersection of the pairs of opposite sides lie in one straight line. (However, if the opposite sides are parallel then the points will lie in the line at infinity.)

The vertices of the hexagon are A, B, C, D, E, F; they are in an ellipse (conic) and when opposite sides AF and CD, FE and BC, AB and ED are produced, they meet in points X, Y, Z which lie on the same straight line. Pascal called the hexagon his 'mysterium hexagrammicum' (mystic hexagram).

This discovery brought Blaise, a boy of sixteen, to the attention of the French and many other European scientists and mathematicians, including Descartes and Fermat, and suggested to them the promise of a new mathematician of the first rank.

At almost the same time as Blaise made his triumph with his geometry, Etienne made a serious blunder. Etienne's fortune was invested in a kind of government bond and Cardinal Richelieu reduced the value of these bonds by one third in order to finance his war. The elder Pascal protested to such an extent that he ruffled the feathers of Seguier, the Chancellor and a *Lettre de cachet* was issued. The warrant for his

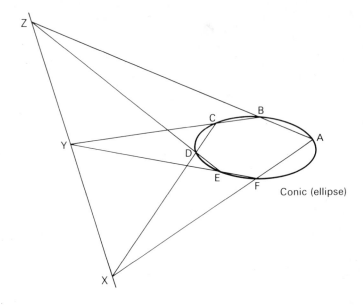

Conic (ellipse)

arrest could have placed Etienne in the Bastille but he fled to Clermont in time to prevent this.

The situation was, however, saved by Blaise's younger sister Jacqueline who is remembered as a girl of intelligence and charm. By means of a plot hatched with Etienne's friends, Jacqueline was selected to play the leading part in a play given by children to entertain Richelieu and his friends in his home. Jacqueline played her part well; the play was a success and also her manner so attracted the Cardinal that during a pleasant interview she was able to persuade him to drop the charges against her father.

An equally important sequel to this event came a few months later. Although he had angered the Cardinal, Etienne was a civil servant of ability and distinction. This had somehow registered with Richelieu during their disagreement and Etienne was recalled to service with the particularly important task of taking charge of the tax collection at Rouen; Richelieu was still in need of money for his religious hostilities and viewed both Etienne and Rouen as a means of improving his finances.

In 1640 the family moved to Rouen and stayed there for

the next seven years. Etienne was very much occupied with the accountancy and statistics of his tax gathering as vast quantities of arithmetic entered into his daily life from all directions and probably kept him busy for most of his waking hours. Blaise, like some before him and many since, was taken by the sheer drudgery of the work which his father, and presumably himself, was put to, and he determined to find a way to save these labours. To this end he set himself the task of constructing a calculating machine.

The idea of a device which could add, subtract, multiply and divide and carry digits from one column to the next was conceived during his first year in Rouen. To carry out his plan he needed a design, materials and craftsmen to build the actual machine. Unlike Schickard's calculator, which was largely wooden, his was to be made of metal. He engaged craftsmen in the town and his first machine was finished in 1642. This did not accomplish the whole of his scheme: he had to settle for just the operations of addition and subtraction, together with the facility for carrying figures. During the next few years Pascal worked on his device, producing improved models with each attempt. Some were intended for the addition and subtraction of numbers, others were designed to carry out the same operations with money. These included mechanisms to cope with twenty units for the sous and twelve units for the deniers. Pascals called his creation the 'Pascaline' and up to about 1652 over fifty models were made. Some of these still exist, including two in the possession of the Conservatoire des Arts et Metiers, Paris. One of these is an eight figure machine with registers for sous and deniers; the other is more basic, with only six figures. There is a copy of the latter model in the Science Museum, London.

This slightly simpler machine is a box with six sets of pin-wheels and cylinders. each of the cylinders is marked with the figures 0 to 9. One figure of each cylinder is viewed through a small hole in the box. Each pin-wheel is also connected to a dial on the front of the box, which has ten notches. With a peg, the dial, and hence the pin-wheel, can be moved forward or backward a number of notches, which correspond to tenths of the pin-wheel. The pin-wheels are connected to the cylinders, so as a wheel is advanced or retarded so is the corresponding cylinder and hence the number visible. To add two numbers, 3 and 2 say: one number 3, is set on the cylinder, again by means of a dial, and the other is added by turning the front (pin-wheel) dial from 2 to 0, the number 5 then appears through the viewing hole. To perform subtraction on Pascal's machine it was necessary to move a bar over the addition viewing holes, at the same time exposing similar figures, this time written the opposite way round on the cylinder, through similar holes above them. This was because the automatic carrying device, the *sautoir*, only worked one way. 3–2 could then be performed with the same operations as for addition but this time with the cylinder figures moving from 3 to 1 (instead of from 3 to 5). To carry out realistic calculations most of the cylinders and dials would be operated in this fashion.

Pascal's machine was a success. There is no more sure sign of success than plagiarism, and this is precisely what happened. The ingenious mechanism was of interest to all capable craftsmen and no doubt Blaise's workmen discussed it with others of their trade. One watchmaker in Rouen is said to have constructed a clever copy from the details he gathered in this way and he then tried to pass it off further afield as his own invention. Blaise was annoyed as much by the fact that some people believed it was the creation of a mere watchmaker as he was at having his design stolen. In 1645 he applied to Chancellor Segnier for the sole right to make his machine; this with the *privilege du roi* (privilege of the king) amounted to a patent. Lest the Chancellor should still be annoyed by his father's unfortunate wrath at having his securities devalued, Blaise sought to placate him by making him a present of one of his calculators. Exclusive rights for the machine were forthcoming and Pascal set about marketing it.

The financial success he expected was not forthcoming. He found that he could not make his device at a price merchants and the like were prepared to pay. He travelled quite widely and gave demonstrations but few sales were effected. The standard model, which he produced in 1652, was priced at one hundred livres, a considerable sum of money. In the hope of some business he made at least one further gift: that of one of his machines to Queen Christiana of Sweden. The famous René Descartes served this sovereign as mathematics tutor until his untimely death in 1650 from pneumonia, brought on by having to give his instruction in a damp and unhealthy palace during the cold of the night. Blaise thought that the royal lady's predisposition to mathematics might have gained him some goodwill and eventually some buyers, but none came.

Towards the conclusion of the main development work on his calculator in 1645, Blaise found a new interest. News was brought to him of Torricelli's work on the pressure of the air. Blaise, together with his father and Pierre Petit, who had first learned of the Italian's experiments, repeated these using a four foot tube filled with mercury. Apart from the surprise at the mercury freely rising up the tube, there was great interest in the nature of the apparently empty space above the liquid. 'Was this truly a vacuum?' they thought. But they well knew that nature abhorred a vacuum. The experiment was performed many times with tubes of different lengths and with different liquids. Blaise soon took charge of the experiments, with Petit and Etienne content to follow the young Pascal. They found that the height of the liquid was constant at whatever angle the tube was inclined. Blaise devised methods for obtaining large voids and gradually the experimenters became convinced that indeed the space above the barometer liquid was a vacuum, although many hours of experimentation and much ingenuity had gone into their work. One of the clever techniques they devised involved what we now recognise as the syringe, now so common in medical and dental surgeries.

The Pascal experiments were not the only ones being performed in this area; news of Torricelli's discovery had stimulated the work of other scientists and so Blaise was determined to report his results as soon as possible. In October 1647 he published his *Expériences Nouvelles Touchant La Vide* which was intended as an abridgement of a proposed much longer treatise on the nature of the vacuum. A month previously he had been visited by the great René Descartes himself, who had come to learn more of his mathematics and of his scientific experiments, The first meeting was somewhat marred by the presence of Roberval, who was intent on being a kind of master of ceremonies. The following day Pascal and Descartes talked in private and a much more fruitful discussion took place. It was a mark of recognition that the great French intellect should visit the enfant terrible of European science.

In November 1647 Blaise thought out a conclusive experiment to show that the pressure of the air was the sole cause of the strange behaviour of the mercury in his tubes. The experiment was to make numerous observations of the same barometer tube of mercury at the foot and the summit of a mountain in the same day to discover whether the level of the liquid was the same at the different heights. Pascal's confirmation would be: if the height of the mercury was greater at the top of the mountain than at its base, then the pressure of the atmosphere would be the cause of the void above the mercury column.

To carry out such an experiment would be an arduous task. Pascal, for most of his life, suffered the most abominable ill health. Not only did he suffer, often almost continuously, the tormenting headaches due to the malformation of his cranium, but some other disorder affected his stomach and other vital organs. One of the pieces of advice Descartes gave him during his visit was to rise from his bed late in the morning, and only when he felt sufficiently well, carry out his daily duties. In the actual experiment, it was Florin Perier, the husband of his sister Gilberte, who made the measurements. The mountain chosen was the Puy De Dome but the ascent was delayed until September 1648 because of time and weather. In the event, two similar tubes of mercury were used; one remained at the foot of the mountain while Perier measured the height of the mercury at five different levels. The conclusion was that the mercury column decreased steadily with increasing height. Pascal prepared two further treatises on his experiments; these concerned air pressure, but they were not published until after his death.

During the early part of 1654, he worked on mathematics. Two projects took his attention; one was investigations into conic sections, like those which had given him his first success with Pascal's theorem, and the production of a treatise on their geometry (now unfortunately lost). The other was suggested by his friend the Chevalier de Mere, who was much disposed to gaming. De Mere asked questions about gambling, including how the winnings should be apportioned if a game of dice was interrupted before it reached it natural conclusion. Pascal solved this and the other questions of his friend. He also sent the problems to the mathematician Fermat in Toulouse, who confirmed his answers. In the course of his investigations, Pascal used and investigated the nature of the well-known triangle of numbers, which is now known as 'Pascal's Triangle', but it is, in fact, of very much earlier origin.

```
                1
              1   2   1
            1   3   3   1
          1   4   6   4   1
        1   5  10  10   5   1
      1   6  15  20  15   6   1
    1   7  21  35  35  21   7   1
```
Pascal's Triangle

From his work on this subject he was very close to the discovery of the binomial theorem, which was later found by Sir Isaac Newton. The Triangle is still taught as a way of calculating the coefficients of the shorter expansions of binomials. He also used the Triangle in his work on the formula for the sums of powers of consecutive integers. From his investigations of this series he derived the equivalent of the formal for integration

$$\int_0^t x^n \, dx = \frac{t^{n+1}}{n+1}.$$

Indeed, Pascal was one of the mathematicians whose research in areas in which calculus was to become a powerful tool inspired the work of Leibniz on integration. Pascal, himself, had made very definite progress and had he lived longer he might well have succeeded in finding the calculus before either Newton or Leibniz.

Throughout his life he was deeply concerned with religion both at the level of devotion, and at the higher levels of doctrine and theology. He was much attracted to the religious life and followed its precepts without becoming drawn into taking Holy Orders, although he played a part in encouraging his sister Jacqueline to enter a convent in the religious community at Port Royal, a few miles from Paris. However, there was still some ambivalence in his attitude. There were periods when he erred towards a fashionable social life and others, during the later part of his brief life, when he shunned worldly activities, including his scientific and mathematical pusuits as well as comforts and pleasures. His religious activities went deeper than a drift towards increased devotion, because he also became increasingly involved in doctrinal matters and Church politics.

The devotional side of his Catholicism came to a climax with the happenings of the night of Monday 23rd November 1654. Pascal was suffering from a new bout of ill health. During the course of the evening he studied St. John's Gospel, from which he sought the power to overcome his distress. Between half past ten and half past twelve (he timed it carefully) he experienced a divine event. The normal feelings of his senses disappeared and an apparently timeless void took their place, in which he experienced religious ecstasy. In another person this might have been called a conversion, but he was already a strong devotee. His experience was of such power and strength that it rose above all his previous Christian feelings to the extent that he immediately felt compelled to write it down on paper. The following day he copied it on to parchment, and had both accounts sewn into his doubtlet, where they stayed, next to his heart, until they were discovered after his death. One cannot help feeling that there was a strong connection between this event and the nature of his illness, together with its recurrence in a particularly strong form at that time. To Pascal, however, it settled the direction in which he was to live much of the remainder of his life. His wordly life in the salons of Paris was now forsaken and he turned his mind even further towards his faith.

Another version of his conversion, which comes from Voltaire, and is perhaps more fantasy than fact, involves an accident at the Neuilly Bridge across the Seine. One day in 1654 Pascal was driving a large carriage pulled by six horses. On crossing the Seine, either he, or the horses, misjudged the dimensions of the bridge and the two leading animals plunged over the parapet. By quickly cutting the harness, Pascal was saved from a watery end but at the expense of the horses. The fear of his imminent death was such that it brought about his conversion. This event perhaps explained his increasingly devout behaviour, since his ecstatic experience was unknown until after his death. Voltaire, the great French wit, no doubt embellished what was probably a fairly common occurrence when large horse-drawn vehicles crossed narrow bridges.

His conversion was not quite as simple as it may seem; Pascal did not really have the temperament for the monkish life. Not only was he a man with a volatile temper and a personality that did not entertain fools gladly, but he was a person whose knowledge and intellectual sense would not be stifled. His next major activity was to be a religious fight.

Port Royal was the centre of the Jansenists, the followers of the deceased Catholic Bishop of Ypres, Cornelius Jansen. Jansen had written a lengthy work on St. Augustine in which a particular interpretation was given to the notion of Grace. According to Jansen, Grace was bestowed as a gift by God on a few people who found it irresistible, but the vast majority of people did not receive Grace and were doomed. One of the leading orders in the Catholic Church, and particularly strong in France, was the Society of Jesus. The Jesuits, priests of this order, took the view that Grace was there for all Christians to aspire to, and that salvation was there for them all. The Papacy and the rulers of France were particularly influenced by the Jesuits and a religious struggle, which the Jesuits were bound to win, broke out between them and the Jansenists. This struggle is as fascinating as it was bewildering and unfair, but its importance to us lies in the fact that Pascal sided with the Jansenists and fought their cause, largely through his writings, when the leaders of this movement were subjected to ridicule, dishonour and demotion within the Catholic Church.

In his clash with the Jesuits, Pascal wrote open letters to a bogus friend in the provinces describing their attitudes, political and otherwise, as well as their theology, and particularly their treatment of his Jansenist friend Arnauld. He was wise enough to write them under the pseudonym of Louis de Montalte, for their material was sufficiently inflammatory to put him in the Bastille. They were printed by the Jansenists themselves at Port Royal and by sympathetic printers who gambled their liberty on a principle. Eventually the eighteen letters were bound together and have come down to us as the classic of French literature *Lettres Provinciales*.

Along with his increasing devotion went increasing agony;

severe toothache now became a major source of torment. Pascal, who abandoned his mathematical investigations for long periods, is said, by his sister Gilberte, to have sought solace and relief from his toothache by returning to his first interest, geometry. This is reputed to be the start of his work in 1658 on the cycloid, the path of a point on the circumference of a circle as it rolls along a horizontal surface. The calculation of the area, centre of gravity and other characteristics of this curve had long been a problem in mathematics. It was both topical and a subject in which mathematicians of the time were well versed. In the course of his investigations, Pascal found answers to the questions that bothered the mathematical community. The cycloid, however, was only a vehicle for his methods, they were applicable to curves generally. The area, and the related problem of the centre of gravity, was attacked using rectangular strips of the area under the curve; this idea led towards integration and was used later by Leibniz.

Pascal was so pleased with his success that he did not publish his results and only let a few of his friends share the secrets of his discoveries. Instead, he organised a contest; a mathematical challenge in which the mathematicians of France and the rest of Europe were invited to submit solutions to the problems of the cycloid which he had just vanquished. The time allowed for this was three months, after which he would give his own solutions. There were to be two prizes; the first of forty pistoles, the second of twenty. Pascal showed his guile by giving challenge in the name of Amos Dettonville, an anagram of Louis de Montalte of the *Lettres Provinciales*. Many prospective solutions were sent in, including those from Huygens and Wren (later Sir Christopher). The most complete ones came from Wallis, a famous English mathematician and Lalouvere, a Jesuit from Toulouse. In the end, neither man's entry was good enough for the award of the prizes and Pascal dismissed their claims to them in his *Lettres de A. Dettonville*, later he published *Histoire de roulette* containing his own solution.

It was from about this time that his health began to deteriorate markedly. The pains of his body that at one time he could ignore or subdue by intellectual activity now refused to go away. He became increasingly taken up with devotional and other religious matters. Part of his time was spent at Port Royal. From 1660 he largely stopped travelling and disposed of his carriage and horses. His days were filled with meditation, and he became increasingly concerned for the poor and the distressed. As well as organising collections for the needy, he gave the very practical help of taking a poor family into his own home.

Throughout much of the later part of his life he wrote down the thoughts which resulted from his meditations. These were later published as the *Pensées*. He wrote and planned many other works of devotional, practical and scientific natures other than those that have been mentioned.

In June 1662 his illness again became severe. His doctors thought that he was less ill than he believed. However, he did not recover and his poor health continued throughout the summer. On the 17th August he was in terrifying agony with a headache. His doctors diagnosed this as migraine and reported that his life was not in danger. His sister, Gilberte, with whom he was living, was not convinced. She arranged for a priest to spend the night with them. At midnight Pascal was again seized with great pain and appeared to die. However, when the priest entered the room, he opened his eyes and received the priest's blessing. Afterwards he suffered convulsions and died in the early morning.

CHAPTER THREE

Gottfried Wilhelm Leibniz

PASCAL WAS not the only person of the time to show an interest in saving the labour involved in calculating. At the time when he gave up his attempts to find buyers for his machines, a man named **Moreland** was working under royal patronage in England to produce the same sort of things.

Sir Samuel Moreland was born at Sulhamstead-Bannister, near Reading in 1625. His father, Thomas Moreland, was a clergyman and encouraged his talented son in his academic pursuits. Samuel received his education first at Winchester School and then at Magdalen College, Cambridge. In all he spent ten years at this ancient university, but left without taking a degree. However, he cannot have been without talent, for he soon became secretary to Oliver Cromwell. His skill in politics or deception must have been considerable because he later became Master of Mechanics to King Charles II. The rest of his life was spent in devising and inventing mechanical contraptions, many of which were useful and of subsequent importance.

Moreland made three calculating machines. The first, which dates from 1664, was to calculate trigonometric functions and data of triangles. It consists of a series of rods, scales and toothed wheels which can be operated to produce a model of any triangle, from which sine, cosine and tangent as well as the angles themselves can be read off.

A calculator which dates from 1666 was intended for addition and subtraction. It is a small device, about the same size as a modern electronic pocket calculator. The instrument was intended for calculations involving money and because of

Gottfried Wilhelm Leibniz. (Photo: *Science Museum, London*.)

this it has dials and wheels for farthings, pence, shillings, units, tens, hundreds, thousands and tens of thousands. There are eight dials in which figures on a wheel can be set to a datum position using a peg. As the dials are rotated an indicator advances one space with each turn of the corresponding wheel. All except the farthings (4), the pence (12) and the shillings (20) rotate once in ten digits. In fact, the indicators are little more than revolution counters and the skill is in reading the answers. The indicator above the farthings dial shows the number of pence accrued from adding odd farthings, the dial above the pence indicates the number of shillings from odd pence, the number above the shillings shows the number of pounds from odd shillings and so on through the pound dial. To get the final total for an addition it is necessary to add the numbers shown by the indicators to that made up from the figures on the dials. Subtraction can be carried out by moving the wheels and the dials anticlockwise instead of clockwise, but certain differences will introduce complications since there is no device for carrying farthings, pence, shillings or tens in either direction. A calculator of this kind could obviously have its uses in a busy exchequer, but, as with Pascal's machine, a person skilled in figures would probably outrun it unless he had very fast fingers and, in the case of subtraction, an agile brain. This machine, though useful, was not really in the same league as his trigonometrical mechanism when it was operated by an astronomer or mathematician.

His third instrument, as far as I know, now exists only as a description in his book *The Description and Use of Two Arithmetical Instruments*, 1673. This multiplying machine was made about the same time as his adding machine and it was presented to Charles II in 1666. His 'Machina Nova Cyclologica ProMultiplicatione' as he called it was a complicated and intricate set of Napier's Bones, the cylinders of Schott's version having been replaced by discs. To operate the instrument the correct discs had first to be selected and then placed in the required position. Again, reading the parts of the answer was not as simple a task as we would hope for now. A further set of discs could be used for the extraction of square, cube and fourth roots. Then the parts of the answer either had to be added to his adding machine, or else collected in the usual way.

So the gifts from the 'Kings tinkerer' may have been interesting curiosities and important steps in the development of the computer, but they were scarcely of great practical importance.

Moreland spent the remainder of his life constructing intricate inventions. He lived near the Thames in Hammersmith, London and constructed a pump and filtering device which brought clean, fresh water from a dirty part of the Thames into his own garden and for the use of passers-by. He even left a tablet on the side of his house which suggested that he thought very little of anyone who would not give a drink of water to a traveller or tinker.

The Master of the King's Mechanics cannot have claimed a very high stipend, or Moreland somehow incurred Charles' displeasure, for after going blind he died in poverty, even though he was well known to the king and apparently highly regarded by the Archbishop of Canterbury. Sir Samuel Moreland died at his home in Hammersmith on the 30th December 1695.

No doubt Moreland's machines, which are now in the Science Museum, South Kensington, were known in England at the time, but whether news of them spread quickly to continental Europe is not known. Certainly, the next character in the history of the computer, Leibniz, knew of Pascal's machine, but whether he knew of Moreland's at the time of his own interest in such matters is doubtful.

Leibniz was a man of great fame within his own lifetime, and has remained so ever since his death for his work in mathematics, history, philosophy and statecraft. His machine formed only a small aspect of his life, but it is a very important step in the development of automatic calculation.

Gottfried Wilhelm **Leibniz** was born in Leipzig on the 21st June 1646, two years before the end of the Thirty Years War. He was largely protected from the despair being suffered by most Germans because of the elevated position of his family. For three generations they had served the administration of Saxony. They were comfortably rich, well-connected and clever. Leibniz's father was professor of moral philosophy at the University of Leipzig and a judge. As a child Gottfried was talented, with a strong interest in history, which has been attributed to his father. However, the older Leibniz died when his son was only six years old, so his personal influence could not have been very great. However, his father's library remained and was available to him. Also he grew up amongst similar families in a university community. The talent of the young Leibniz must have been encouraged from many quarters, although this attention may not always have been welcome.

He attended school briefly in Leipzig, but he found that he could learn more without help from others. From eight years old onwards he studied first Latin and later Greek. When he tired of these he returned to history. In his later childhood he explored the arts of logic and clear thinking and then settled upon law for his university studies. Whether or not this was by whim or grand design is not known. Later he shunned the possibility of a university career to engage in statecraft, and the law has always been considered an excellent preparation for such activities.

At the age of fifteen he began his studies in law at the University of Leipzig. He found the work so easy that he spent much of his time studying the works of Kepler, Galileo and Descartes. At this time astronomy and physics were regarded as a branch of philosophy, and it is not unreasonable to see these studies of Leibniz as arising from his interest in philosophy generally. To understand the natural philosophy of these men an understanding of mathematics was needed. This was the purpose of his journey to the University of Jena in 1663. He felt that Erhard Weigil, the professor of mathematics at Jena, had more to offer than could be obtained at Leipzig. Whatever Weigil's merits for Leibniz, the man has since gone into oblivion in the history of mathematics. When Leibniz returned to Leipzig he continued his legal studies and was set for his doctorate in 1666, but the Leipzig professors were not prepared for this. They refused him the opportunity to take the degree on the grounds that he was too young. There must have been more to it than this. Leibniz was clever, perhaps too clever. Either he had upset the faculty in some way or else his brilliance overshone theirs and they were not prepared to display their own ignorance. Certainly, the young student had no difficulty in submitting the thesis for his doctorate to the University of Aldorf, near Nuremburg. The degree was conferred on the 5th November of the same year. Leibniz distinguished himself so well that he was asked to accept the professorship of law within the university. He declined the invitation explaining 'that he had very different things in view'.

His *De arte combinatoria* which he described as his 'schoolboy's essays' was written in 1666 and it was the synthesis of much of his philosophical thinking. Since his teens he had been taken with the need for clear thinking. If not quite obsessed with the elimination of the imponderables and uncertainties of discussion and writing, he was certainly annoyed by them. It is natural that a youth should strive for perfection before the practicalities and shortcomings of life and age beat him, but Leibniz was astute enough to succeed in part. As has been said he was a scholar of philosophy and the idea of the thirteenth century exponent of this art, Raymond Lull, that philosophy, logic and the sciences depend upon certain basic concepts or categories attracted him. Leibniz took the idea further. He suggested that there could be a universal language of categories in which it was possible to represent any argument or conjecture in terms of these basic concepts. Having done that, there would be a kind of logical algebra by which the statements could be simplified, finally leaving the truth of the matter apparent in symbols, only requiring to be transferred again into everyday language. This idea can be seen to be scientifically interesting as well as of importance to fruitful thinking. It can be seen as a culmination of logic and embryonically as the beginning of a language, which, because of its lack of ambiguity, is suitable for machines and eventually the computer.

Leibniz's place in the history of the computer is usually thought to be for his calculating machine, but he also made important contributions to the idea of computer design, 'thought' and language. As we will see, George Boole's logic, which is more easily recognisable as being important to the design and operation of electronic computers, was directly influenced by this portion of Leibniz's philosophy.

Although Leibniz's language was not fully worked out in terms of syntax, nor was his algebra sufficiently formulated, he designed symbols for 'and', 'or', implication, class inclusion and class equivalence. This essay, written while he was still twenty, was only one of his many achievements. However, it must rank as one of his most important, even though it has not been completely realised, nor has the progress that has been made been achieved by him. He had originally felt that he and some talented assistants might have accomplished the task in five years; instead, at the end of his life he regretted that he had not returned to it.

The following year he stayed in Nuremberg and attended to his developing interest in alchemy with the members of the Rosicrucian order of the town. The secret society of the Rosicrucians still exists today.

His thesis for his doctorate was concerned with a new way of teaching law. It attracted great attention among those concerned with legal matters and so that its content should become more readily available, it was suggested that he should have it printed. The printed essay came into the hands of the Elector-Archbishop of Mainz, who then sent for the author. After a long and profitable interview, the youthful Leibniz was offered a job. Basically he was to be a mixture of legal expert, a dogsbody, troubleshooter and envoy. His immediate task was to modify the legal code of the state, to make it more appropriate to the time and to suit his employer's desires. He was, however, to do more than this. Politics then, as at any other time, was a mixture of many ingredients from intrigue, deceit, knowing who and who not to see, discovering the right facts and suppressing the wrong ones, to seeing that meetings were arranged at the right time and the appropriate words were spoken. At all these tasks, Leibniz was a master, and his cleverness and discretion were well rewarded.

To do the bidding of his employer, Leibniz had to travel extensively. The roads that existed were at best difficult, often rain made them impassable because of flooding or so muddy that the carriage wheels stuck and the horses shied. The aftermath of rains and snows left hard, sunbaked ruts that rattled the bones of travellers. Staying overnight, often in strange inns, with untested standards of food, comfort and cleanliness cannot have been conducive to good temper and firm health. Leibniz must have travelled hundreds of thousands of miles under these circumstances, yet wherever he went, he worked. He read and wrote during the ricketty carriage journeys, and also in the badly lit rooms of the hostelries in which he stayed. During these journeys he hatched all manner of new and wonderous things in mathematics and philosophy, as well as seeing to the paperwork of the Elector-Archbishop's business. Many of his best notions came out of these inclement circumstances. When he died he left vast piles of papers, many of which were scraps obtained from a casual source and covered with the jottings made during his jouneys. It is only in the present century that efforts have been made to put much of this work in order. His mathematical writings alone fill a dozen volumes.

The political adventures of Leibniz were varied and numerous. He occasionally took on the most unlikely tasks, ones which could have easily come from the exploits of Baron Münchhausen or Don Quixote. One of the earliest of these was to persuade the King of France to invade Egypt. His master, like many German rulers, was restricted by fear of the possible actions of Louis XIV. Leibniz conceived the idea for the proposed invasion himself and attempted to interest the French ruler in it rather than a similar action against Germany. It was a bold suggestion, but the resourceful envoy was told, via the courtesies of statesmanship, that holy wars had gone out of fashion. The proposed stratagem lay hidden for over a century, only to be discovered by Napoleon in 1803 when he occupied Hanover. This notion of Leibniz rather pre-empted Napoleon's own Egyptian expedition of 1799.

During his time with the Elector of Mainz, he set about developing his idea for a calculating machine for he believed that 'It is unworthy of excellent men to lose hours like slaves in the labour of calculation, which could safely be passed on to anyone else if machines were used'. This statement was made in 1671, when he began his work. Previously he had studied Pascal's machine (and his other work) and was quite impressed with its mechanism, but it was his desire to make a device which would perform multiplication and division as well as addition and subtraction. Leibniz' machine was to be of two parts: a 'Pascaline' for the simple operations, and a part utilising his own key idea for multiplication and division. This new development was the stepped wheel, a device so obvious and ingenious, that it had the qualities of beauty and endurance far beyond Leibniz' time. It has nine wheels on one shaft, the first with nine teeth, the second with eight and so on, so arranged that an engaging gear wheel could be turned by any number of teeth from one to nine respectively, and after the adjacent engaging teeth had acted there would be no further mechanical contact for the rest of the revolution.

In 1672 Leibniz went to Paris. Although he was still in the employment of the Elector and carried out missions of importance, he began to study mathematics deeply. With the help of Christian Huygens, a scientist and mathematician, he caught up on the mathematical developments which had escaped his attention either through his complete ignorance of their existence or because they had taken place in parts of Europe with which he had little contact. During this time he generally sharpened his wits in this subject and developed his skills as a mathematician. Until then he had been a lawyer and philosopher with an interest in the subject; from this period which lasted until 1676, he emerged as a supreme adept at mathematics.

His affairs took him across the English Channel to London in 1673. Once there, he set about meeting the English mathematicians. At a meeting of the Royal Society, he demonstrated the principles of his calculating machine. No doubt, if he was not already acquainted with Moreland's work before this, he learned of it at this time. It would seem that the members of this illustrious body were so taken with the ideas, and possibly some models, of his calculator that they made him a foreign member of the Society.

This year was also the time of the invention which is remembered by mathematicians above all his other triumphs and discoveries. He was studying the work of Pascal on the cycloid, and in particular the letter of Amos Dettonville entitled 'Traite des sinus du quant de cercle'. From his studies he realised that the tangent to a curve depends upon the ratio of the differences of the distances on the y and x axes as they become smaller and smaller, that, although these quantities, which he called dx and dy, might become infinitesimally small, their ratio was preserved as a definite number without being similarly reduced. This was the birth of his differential calculus. He also realised that the calculation of the area under a curve, or the quadrature of a curve, was obtainable from the sum of the unlimited set of infinitesimally small rectangles from which this area was made up. To crown these two momentous achievements, he realised that the processes of differentiation and integration (quadrature) were related and that, in fact, one was the inverse of the other.

Sir Isaac Newton's formulation of the calculus took place in 1665–66, seven years before that of Leibniz. The two men had very different expressions for essentially the same ideas and both seemed reluctant to publish them. The first into print was Leibniz in 1684. Under the title *Novus methodus pro maximus et minimus, itemque tangentibus, qua nec irrationales quantitates moratur'* (*A New Method for Maxima and Minima, and also for Tangents, which is not Obstructed by Irrational Quantities*) he gave the formulae for differentiation of powers, products and quotients: $dx^n = nx^{n-1}$,

$d(xy) = xdy + ydx$ and $d(\dfrac{x}{y}) = \dfrac{(ydx - xdy)}{y^2}$, which are

only slightly different from the ones in use in most schools and colleges at present. This was not all: in 1686 he published his notions of integration or quadrature, and explained in *Acta Eruditorum*, a journal which he had founded somewhat earlier, how it was the inverse of differentiation.

This cornerstone of much of higher mathematics, although a momentous and independent achievement for both Newton and Leibniz, was to be the cause of emotional unrest for both of them. Their achievements in the whole of learning were recognised by the French Academy of Sciences who made them their joint first foreign members.

During Leibniz' sojourn in Paris his employer died and he then entered the employ of the Brunswick family, the House of Hanover. He stayed in the service of this House until his death but served three successive dukes. At first he acted in much the same way as he had served his previous master, but in 1680 he was given, amongst other things, the specific post of family librarian at Wolfenbüttel and the very important task of writing the history of the famous and illustrious family. It was not, however, to be a mere superficial history book detailing the family's glories; it was to include a wealth of detail of kinship and lineage. All the connections with the courtly and royal families of Europe were to be fully explored. Those hinted at were to be extensively researched and those which were only possible were to be accepted if they could be beneficial. Past alliances and relationships which could be detrimental to the family's future were to be discredited. The interweaving of even the royal families was so complex that the unravelling of the Brunswick connections was an arduous task which eventually proved to be impossible.

In the course of his genealogical investigations, Leibniz went to Rome, to ascertain whether or not the Brunswicks were connected with the Italian Estes family. Being such a notable person, he was called to an audience with the Pope and along with the delicacies of the occasion His Holiness made a proposition to Leibniz. He wished him to be librarian to the Vatican. This was more than an honour or tribute to his skill as a librarian; it was an unbelievable invitation. Leibniz was not a Catholic and the Vatican library was, even then, of massive size and contained books and manuscripts to which the multitude of the Catholic faith and the world generally had long since been denied access because of their embarrassing contents. Although Leibniz would be required to enter the faith, this was a tremendous compliment to his skills of tact, discretion and diplomacy. And it was more; the material which he would control would give him such power that the Church authorities must have had complete trust that he would adjust his scruples according to the moment. By their nature, church and state politics necessitate a flexibility of attitude; but the Pope's proposition represented a very definite lapse on his part unless he was very sure of his ground.

In the event, the proposition was not accepted. Leibniz had a different plan. He attempted, by exercising considerable diplomacy in the arrangement of meetings and congresses, to re-unite the Roman and Protestant Churches. In the 1680s this reunification was a definite possibility, but it failed. That he should undertake this course at the expense of a powerful position with the very definite possibility of a cardinal's hat (and how Leibniz must have itched to get his hands on the forbidden writings and suppressed knowledge) suggests that he expected to gain something very valuable. As must be gathered by now, he was not the most honest of men!

As regards his honesty, a strange conundrum emerges. The great Jewish philosopher Benedict de Spinoza, whose whole philosophy was dominated by the notion of God, suffered at the hands of Leibniz where his writing on ethics was concerned. Leibniz seems to have left Paris with part of Spinoza's unpublished work. The Jew's ideas later turned up again in Leibniz' writings. Whether this was plagiarism or the expression of sympathetic ideas is a matter of conjecture, there have been many other instances of simultaneous discoveries, but . . .!

Leibniz was not content with his failure at the complete reunification of the churches; he went on to attempt a reparation between the two major Protestant sects. In the light of history the great man need not have been dismayed at his second failure; a lot more failures and little success at the same task has followed in the three hundred years since his time.

Through all these exploits, Leibniz had been working on his calculating machine. It is doubtful if his efforts were anything approaching continuous. He was more likely to collect ideas and notions from the thoughts and experiences of himself and others. Craftsmanship in the latter part of the seventeenth century was very different from what it is now. This was more than a hundred years before the great metalworking craftsmen emerged in response to the needs of the industrial revolution. Any novel mechanical contraption of Leibniz' time was likely to stretch the capabilities of the metalworkers of the time. This was basically the trouble; Leibniz' ideas of 1671 were sound, but their transmutation into gear wheels which were neither too slack to be inaccurate nor too tight to be immovable was essentially impossible at the time. These problems and the associated phenomena of backlash and accumulated friction were to defeat other pioneers of the computer as well as Leibniz. There must have been many models produced by his mechanics, but the definitive version of his calculator is said to stem from 1694. This carried out the operations it had been designed to perform but it was reputed to have been temperamental, sluggish and prone to sticking. Leibniz was asked by Peter the Great to make one of his devices so that it would be sent to the Emperor of China as a present to show the Orient that the culture of Europe was not without its own novel and intricate mechanisms, and therefore facilitate trade between the two continents.

Among the ideas which Leibniz explored was the binary

system for counting. This system, which is the basic mode of operation of the electrical circuitry of today's computers, was seen in its true light by Leibniz as a great simplifying approach to automatic computation, but it required too many moving metal parts to be of use to him. He was, however, intrigued by the notion and is said to have used it to prove the existence of God to the satisfaction of the Chinese Emperor. Leibniz represented nothing with O and God with 1 and by cunningly suggesting that the world exists therefore it must be 1, he convinced the wily oriental that there is a God. The Emperor must have taken some convincing because Leibniz had four arguments for the existence of God; this is a variation on his ontological argument.

After Leibniz there followed the creations of many mathematicians and mechanics which used Leibniz' ideas, particularly his stepped wheel. The first really practical machine was built and later manufactured and placed on general sale by Chevalier Chas X Thomas de Colman. It is known as the first of a type of calculator called the 'Arithmometer'. This machine appeared around 1820 in its polished form, when the master craftsmen could shape a machine to the exacting requirements needed for a mechanical calculator. It contained the stepped wheel or cylinder based on Leibniz' ideas, but in a form which he could not have hoped to produce.

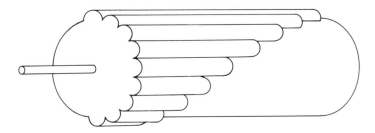

To multiply on this arithmometer, 4031 by 642 for example, the number 4031 is set on 4 slots by turning a wheel. One turn is required for 1, nine for 9 etc., this operation moves an engaging wheel into position to engage with from 0 to 9 of the teeth on the stepped cylinder. The mechanism with the cylinder could be moved from the gear wheel of one dial on to another, and to multiply by 642 it was simply a question of setting this in the correct position relative to 4031 for long multiplication, turning the handle twice, then moving to the next column and turning it four times and finally to the next column amd turning it six times. Obviously Leibniz' invention is of no importance in the age of microcircuits, but it served trade and industry when it was incorporated in nineteenth century calculators.

Throughout the forty-three years he served the House of Hanover, Leibniz continued to develop his own studies and thinking. He developed a worldwide reputation for philosophy, language, history, politics and statesmanship. In 1700 he founded the Berlin Academy of Sciences and became its first president. His knowledge of the intricacies and byways of European history was phenomenal and his list of influential contacts almost endless. Yet there was a major problem that affected him personally and it stemmed from probably his greatest creation, calculus. Leibniz had been in London in 1673 after Newton had made his discoveries in the subject. It was suggested by the English mathematicians that his ideas were merely reconsidered notions of the great Englishman. At about the same time the European mathematicians, notably the Bernoullis, championed Leibniz' cause and accused Newton of purloining his ideas. After all Leibniz did publish first. This argument between the mathematical communities of England and the Continent, which was largely carried on without either Newton or Leibniz, engendered bad feeling in the mathematical world. The international contact between mathematicians, which is essential to the development of their subject, ceased. Leibniz became *persona non grata* in England. This would probably not have worried him under ordinary circumstances, but a well-known change in European history took place in 1714; the Elector of Hanover became George I of England. Consequently, he moved his establishment of counsellors and confidantes to London. But Leibniz was not invited. This lapse on the part of the monarch is usually ascribed to the feud over the calculus, but there may have been other reasons. Would it have been good politics for a foreign noble accepting an English throne to annoy the members of the influential and covertly powerful Royal Society?

Leibniz was left at home in Hanover, writing the history of

the Brunswick family. By the time of his death on the 14th November 1716 he had reached the year 1005. This incomplete work of the master intellect was considered so important by the family that it was not published until well into the nineteenth century; it had lain forgotten for over a hundred years.

He did not receive the funeral due to an elder statesman of European politics; one of the wisest men the world has ever known was buried with only his attendant and workmen present.

Before leaving Leibniz, a little of his philosophy may be worth recounting. In essence, he believed in an unlimited number of substances which he called 'monads'. These had many curious properties and they made up the whole of the universe. In fact, each one was really a mirror of the universe. One monad did not affect another, yet they made up all things, including our bodies, and therefore were able to act in a kind of unison. There was a hierarchy of monads, with, in the case of a person, the soul being the most senior, yet each monad was itself a soul. Since they made up animate things, some at least of the monads were endowed with means of perception, of senses. According to Leibniz, the space in which we live and move does not exist, but the monads arranged in a particular order experience perceptions and generate a perspective for the senses; this creates what we understand as space. The monads were created by God, and according to Leibniz they play a major part in explaining his existence. The monads are one of Leibniz's most colourful and most difficult concepts.

In a less intellectual way one of his sayings was 'All is for the best in this the best of all possible worlds'. This optimistic philosophy was masterfully satirised by Voltaire, the eighteenth century French writer, in his *Candide* (or Optimism). In the story, Dr. Pangloss is a caricature of Leibniz.

A LA MÉMOIRE DE J. M. JACQUARD.

Né a Lyon le 7 Juillet 1752 Mort le 7 Aout 1834

Joseph Marie Jacquard, portrait woven on silk. (Photo: *British Crown Copyright, Science Museum, London.*)

CHAPTER FOUR

Joseph Marie Jacquard

THE MACHINES constructed by Pascal, Moreland and Leibniz are scarcely recognisable as primitive computers, but perhaps they are easily seen as old-fashioned calculators. From a computer, even an antiquated one, we expect more, we expect it to do not only the work of the operator's head but that of his pencil and paper and much of that of his body. In fact, we expect to be able to give the machine a problem and sit and wait for it to be worked out. Our conception of a computer is an automatic machine. Automation is, of course, not the sole prerogative of computers; it has been in science and industries for centuries.

To trace a little of the history of automation we will take a fruitful analogy. Suppose a person is playing a piano. The output of the piano is, hopefully, a pleasant sound, which compares with the output of a computer or calculator as the answer to our problem. The musician presses the keys of the piano to produce this just as the mathematician presses the keys of his calculator, or perhaps, some time ago, his 'Pascaline'. The pianist has his music and, presumably, the mathematician has a plan of how to process his calculation. Some time before these actions there must be the composition of the music and design of the method of the calculation. Suppose now we substitute a pianola or a barrel organ for the piano. A barrel organ has a metal drum with pegs in it in suitable places so that when it is turned the pegs strike the correct notes to produce the tune. The real part of playing the barrel organ then becomes the construction of the device which orders the tune. Once this is done the monkey can turn the handle (although he rarely did). Automatic musicianship is a long way from the automatic computer but it was, perhaps, the start of automation.

Perhaps the earliest mechanism of this type was that of a pegged cylinder used in musical boxes, where the pegs struck in the correct sequence a few notes to produce a well-known tune. This device was first developed in the fourteenth century and is still made today. This is just a scaled down version of the organ grinder's barrel. As time passed, master craftsmen made the cylinders, often of brass, so that they could reproduce complex pieces of music to a high standard. This art did not end there, all kinds of mechanical novelties were produced; sometimes whole bands or even small orchestras made mechanical music by this method, and mechanical toys (for the very rich) executed all kinds of complicated manoeuvers.

Very often the masters of silversmithing and instrument making who produced the automatons were ignorant of or simply not interested in applying these ideas to such industry as there was. It was therefore, some time before these ideas were seen in the factory, but as usual, it was economics which eventually caused the advancement of industrial automation. The weaving of patterned fabrics was a slow and laborious process, and consequently, expensive, with only the rich being able to afford the fine products. In the early eighteenth century, the French silk making industry used what were known as draw looms. The weaver controlled the shuttle which passed the weft or cross threads over the longitudinal or warp threads which formed the patterned silk material. The weaver's assistant or apprentice pulled cords which lifted particular warp threads to allow the shuttle to pass underneath. This was the heart of the pattern making.

In 1725, Basile **Bouchon**, working in Lyons, the centre of the French silk industry, made the first step. He went two steps ahead of the master jewellers and instrument makers by turning their idea inside out and then applying it to industry. Instead of pegs stuck on a cylinder, he cut holes in a tape. Needles attached to the cords controlling the warps were able to pass through the holes in his perforated tape, which could then be moved on to produce the next line of the pattern. It is believed that only one line of the design at a time could be controlled in this way.

One of the Lyons master weavers of this time was **Falcon**. He worked in collaboration with Bouchon and in 1728, three years after the first device, a new draw loom was built which used cards instead of tape. These cards each had four rows of twenty holes and thus had a very definite advantage over the single row of holes in the tape. Although the cards were strung together, they would not pass through the loom automatically. A 'draw boy' placed the cards, one at a time, in the correct position to impede or allow the passage of the warp needles. Although a loom still required two operators, the weaving process was speeded up and Falcon's loom enjoyed some success; about forty of them are known to have been made. The 'draw boy' was probably one of the first mental casualties of automation. (Was there a Wednesday dress or shawl, perhaps?)

Once started, automation was here to stay, with inventors, industrialists and craftsmen all looking to make improvements. Plainly, if a loom would work with only one operator, or even none, it would be to the advantage of all except the displaced weavers. Jacques **de Vaucanson** sensed the possibilities and after being appointed inspector of silk factories in 1841, applied his skills in this direction. He succeeded completely in making an automatic pattern weaving loom, dispensing with both weavers; however, this was at the expense of the complexity of the designs woven into the silk. He went back to the cylinder. This time it was hollow, with perforations instead of holes, but it was limited by the built-in repetition of the pattern. As the cylinder began each new revolution it repeated the design. The cylinders had a great number of holes and could be changed at appropriate times in the weaving. Vaucanson made a number of other improvements in the weaving industry, some of which are still in use in an updated form. However, his fame really rests with his skill as a maker of automatons. Even as a boy he had shown great skill in this direction and after studying mechanics in Paris, he exhibited in 1736 an automaton which emulated human lip and finger movements with sufficient accuracy to play a flute. He made automatons throughout his life, and few still exist.

It is not uncommon for one person to follow a number of painstaking pioneers who have enjoyed only moderate or partial success and combine and modify their ideas with a more superior and completely workable result. Very often the achievements of the early workers are dwarfed and then forgotten by those who gained the eventual success. This was very much the case with the pattern weaving loom. The limited success of Bouchon, Falcon and Vaucanson was eclipsed by the eminently practical machine of Jacquard.

Joseph Marie **Jacquard** was born in Lyons on the 7th July 1752. His birthplace, a major silk weaving town in the world and the heart of the French industry, was significant since throughout his childhood he was surrounded by people engaged in the tedious and intricate work of weaving fine fabrics. In such a community a child learns the words and the use of the tools of the trade at his mother's knee. Nearly all the young Joseph's friends, relatives and acquaintances had some connection with weaving. His parents made their living as weavers, and throughout the hours of daylight there was little escape from the rattle of looms. Before he was very old he was part of all this activity. First he fetched and carried, and when there was little work for him to do he watched.

As soon as he was old enough to be sufficiently alert, he was employed as a 'draw boy', pulling the cords attached to the warp thread. Much of the early automation of pattern looms in Lyons had either been limited to a few factories or had fallen into disuse from not being as adaptable as it was originally hoped. Certainly the small family establishments could neither find the money for new machines, nor afford to allow them to be idle while engineers and mechanics tinkered with their mechanism in the hope of producing something useful. All this meant that young Joseph had a very tedious time. Many of his friends had little opportunity to leave the silk weaving trade from about seven years old, when they became an important part of the family economy. This was not the case with the young Jacquard. He did not adapt well to the job. He was dazed and dazzled and finally annoyed by the dozens of cords which he had to control. Twelve hours or more of this each day was impossible. Joseph's lack of concentration only served to annoy the weavers he assisted. Probably one of these was his father. So it was decided that he should try his hand at another trade.

First he was apprenticed as a bookbinder, but this also had disadvantages. Always the apprentice or assistant got the tedious jobs. Long hours of sorting and trimming pages did not please Joseph and so he went into the type founding trade. He liked this second choice more and he developed skills and achieved some success as a craftsman. He liked working with metal and went to work as a cutler.

When he was about twenty his father died; his mother had already died a little earlier. Joseph's inheritance was a small house in the village of Cauzon, near Lyons and the family weaving equipment. This was both a time of sadness and the beginning of a period of opportunity. Jacquard knew of the developments in automatic pattern weaving and their advantages and disadvantages. He now had skill in metal working and he set about carrying out his own experiments. The family loom was only a small machine, and Jacquard found it impossible to earn sufficient money by weaving and to also develop his ideas at the same time. Over the years that he worked on his ideas, he spent what little money his father had left him and acquired debts. His pattern loom idea did not get very far, but not for the want of his own industry. Jacquard then returned to metal working to earn his living and settle his debts, but he did not abandon his quest.

About 1790, after many failures, Jacquard conceived the idea which was to work. Unfortunately, success came at a bad time. As the loom was nearing completion, the French Revolution was beginning. Jacquard was quick to side with the Revolutionaries and he fought fiercely in the defence of Lyons. Joseph's son, now a young man, was killed in this action. It was a sad and lonely man who returned home to Cauzon. Jacquard was now within reach of practical success. When the confusion subsided, he began work on his loom. His early success was soon noticed and the City of Lyons allowed him a room in the Palace of Fine Arts, provided that he instructed apprentices without a fee.

In 1801 he completed his machine for weaving nets. This loom combined the inventions of Bouchon, Falcon and Vaucanson. His new machine has been constructed in response to a prize being offered by the Society of Arts in London for a machine for the automatic weaving of fishing nets. The weavers of Lyons sent him to Paris to demonstrate the machine. Once there he displayed it at the *Conservatoire des Arts et Metiers*. Later he showed it to the authorities from London who were awarding the prize. The prize was eventually his. On the 4th February 1804 he received 3,000 francs and a gold medal from the Society. He was granted a patent for his machine and received an invitation from the Conservatoire to work there on his pattern weaving loom and also to examine one of Vaucanson's machines which they possessed. He left Paris in 1804 and returned to Lyons to take charge of the workhouse. In the year or so in which he held this position he completed a pattern weaving loom which was practical and adaptable to a standard sufficient to make it fully acceptable to the weaving trade.

In 1806 his loom was completely accepted. It was declared public property and Jacquard was awarded a state pension of 3,000 francs for his work together with a royalty on each machine made. He was created a Chevalier de la Légion d'honneur. With Lyons being the principal town for weaving, Napoleon gave possession of all of Jacquard's inventions to the city authorities. The inventor himself returned to Paris to the Conservatoire des Arts et Metiers and carried on developing his pattern weaving loom to achieve even greater flexibility and the ability to weave more extensive and complex patterns.

All was not well, however. The staggering success which his loom now had was felt by the weavers, whose lives he had intended to free from the burden of much needless, tedious work. Instead of two weavers to a loom, only one was needed; the 'draw boy' was redundant. Widescale unemployment in Lyons was the feared outcome of the new device. In 1810 the weavers of Lyons erupted in violence and destroyed the Jacquard looms, and very nearly Jacquard himself. The wood of the machines was sold as fuel and the metal as scrap, and Joseph Jacquard believed that all had been in vain. But only two years later, in 1812, there were over 11,000 drawlooms of this type working in France.

With continuous use in factories some shortcomings became apparent in the machines, but these were corrected by Breton in 1815, and Skola in 1819. France further honoured her great inventor. Pattern weaving had now come of age. Soon Jacquard's ideas spread throughout Europe. Even today, machines for producing fabrics with intricate designs are based on Jacquard looms.

Jacquard lived through the tumult of French politics and the wrath of the Lyons weavers to die at the age of 82 at Oullines on the 7th August 1834.

Throughout this chapter, Jacquard's invention has been called a loom, but part of its practicality was that it was less than this. It was a pattern weaving device which could be adapted to looms which were already in existence. The Jacquard, as it became known, used to sit right on the top of the loom. In his invention Jacquard returned to Falcon's idea of punched cards. However, the new machines used cards capable of controlling many needles. Later, machines typically used 200 to 400 needles. The cards allowed these to pass through the holes or not, as the case may be, in much the same way as had been used by Falcon. This idea was not Jacquard's, but the possibilities for weaving which it opened up were. Typical of the cards used in more modern machines were those of thick, stout card 30 cm long and about 7 cm wide, having 400 holes of about 0·7 cm in diameter. The skill of the weaver now shifted, in part at least, to the design of patterns and the perforation of the cards. Jacquard invented cutting and punching machines for this purpose.

Later, the pioneers of computing saw Jacquard cards in a new light; as stores of information, but stores which could easily transfer this information to the wheels, axles and registers of a machine. As both the master weavers and the early programmers discovered, the quantity of information which could be stored and fed into a machine from these cards was limitless. A portrait of Joseph Jacquard himself woven on a loom and Jacquard required 24,000 cards.

Charles Babbage. (Photo: *Science Museum, London*.)

CHAPTER FIVE

Charles Babbage

UP TO the time of **Babbage**, the pioneers of computers produced nothing more than mechanical calculators. Men such as Pascal and Leibniz had the lessening of the drudgering involved in routine calculations as the purpose for their machines. Nowadays, computers fulfil a role much more involved than this, and the intentions of the early pioneers are satisfied by the electronic calculator. It is not surprising that these two common devices of our society should share a common ancestor, since their purposes are similar; but by design, the calculator is a small portable tool for solving small sets of relatively straightforward problems, while the computer is intended to handle or generate a large mass of data and determine results and solutions.

It is with Babbage that the common development of the two machines divides. He introduced the notion of a device which can obey instructions and mechanically carry out on its own a sequence of instructions, solving automatically problems of some complexity, and repeating without prompting the same sequence of operations without the intervention of the operator. Babbage's conception of the computer was not, in theory, very much different from the overall plan of modern machines. It had an input, an output, a store, an arithmetic unit and the energy mechanism to drive the machine, the whole of which was controlled by a program. Because of this, Babbage was (at least) the father of the idea of the computer.

Superficially Babbage's life seems dull and humdrum but at a slightly deeper level it is exciting and enigmatic. So many events in his life turn out to be much more than what they at first appear. Even his birth has a certain strangeness. In his autobiography, which he did not really want to write because he thought that the effort involved could be put to better use and that his life was uninteresting, but which was nevertheless written to humanise the description of his machines, he recounts his early years in London. His birthplace has often been quoted by biographers and editors as Teignmouth, Totnes or just Devonshire. He gives it as London, but until recently it had been believed that he had made a mistake! However it has been recently settled by scholars that his place of birth was Southwark, London and that the event took place on Boxing Day 1791.

His family was not short of money, his father being a successful banker. During his early years he was looked after by a nurse who frequently escorted him around some of the better London streets. This was not without incident, because on one occasion he became separated from the nurse and was temporarily lost. Much later in his life he was almost killed in exactly the same place by a falling roof slate. From these early times he was fascinated by all things mechanical. Mechanical toys were a particular delight, but he always insisted on knowing how they worked to the extent that they always had to be opened to disclose their secrets even if this meant the toys were broken in the process.

When he was five he was stricken with a serious illness, in the course of which he almost died. After the same thing happened five years later he was sent to live with a clergyman who kept a school at Alphington (near Exeter) in Devonshire. During this period he became fascinated by ghost stories, and was successful in frightening older boys with his ghostly pranks. But he became smitten with the possibility of things supernatural. It had been too easy to score over his school fellows! Was there not something more sinister at work than his own childish play? The education he received consisted of a great deal of Christianity with a very liberal helpong of the bad parts of all forms of evil as offered by a personal Devil. To the young Babbage the Devil was a kind of ghost; did he really exist? Babbage was not without either spirit or determination, so he set out to find the answer to his questions. He collected all the knowledge he could find about the Devil; his fascination increased. He set out to conjure up the Prince of Darkness. Babbage sought out the most deserted spot he could find easily: a dark attic. He closed the door behind him. As blood and circles featured strongly in the lore he had collected, he deliberately cut his finger and drew a bloody circle big enough to stand in. He stepped inside this (still calm and clear headed!) and began to recite the Lord's Prayer backwards, a diabolical formula. The young Babbage did not want to make a pact with the Prince of Darkness; all he wanted was confirmation of his existence and perhaps a personal chat! Would the Devil come as a man, a black cat, or perhaps as a raven or bat? Babbage had already opened the window for this latter eventuality. He waited and waited with his calmness evaporating. His fear welled up into a crescendo of paralysis but then it departed sufficiently for him to leave his mystic circle with a hint of disappointment at the absence of any supernatural occurrence. Almost reluctantly, he left the garret and went downstairs, slowly at first but gradually quickening. Considering that Charles was still recovering from his near fatal illness, the event is all the more remarkable. His fascination with supernatural existence did not quite end here. He was still troubled by both the Devil and the truth of the Bible. This is hardly surprising when he must have been subjected to a very raw and naked form of Christianity during most of his waking hours. As his childish concerns about religion subsided, he still retained an interest in ghosts. While an undergraduate at Cambridge, he formed a ghost hunting club. Also, with one of his school friends, Richard Dacres, he made a pact that whoever died first should appear to the other after his death. Dacres died at sea while still a youth. Although Babbage sat up in bed on the night of his friend's death, his would-be spectral visitor did not appear.

After his recovery to full health, he moved back to London and was placed in a boarding school not far from his home. Here he showed the same spirit as before but developed a studious manner. He was attracted to the school's small library. As he liked the arithmetic lessons, he was drawn by the few books on mathematics. He wanted to learn algebra by himself, but it was not taught to the boys and there was no part of the school day when he could study undisturbed material which was not on the curriculum. As before, he was not without resourcefulness. He hatched a plan. Charles sought out one of his comrades who was also a studious boy and suggested that the two of them should get up at three o'clock in the morning and work in the schoolroom until about five-thirty, lighting a fire to keep them warm. This course of study went on successfully for a number of months. What determination! However, the nightly jaunts were discovered by some of the older boys who wanted to join them. Charles did not want this, as he knew that his period of studious quiet would be shattered by the rising spirits emanating from the boys' natural energy. Babbage was able to prevent all except one very determined youth from joining them, but this addition, as expected, led to the downfall of the nightly study sessions. The high point of his stay at the school was the night when he and his school fellows got drunk on a mixture of cognac and treacle.

Most of the rest of Babbage's school years were spent at a small school near Cambridge which was kept by a clergyman. Again, religion featured highly in his studies, but his passion for mathematics remained. For the last few months before going up to Cambridge University he went to stay with a tutor in Totnes. This man coached him in classics only. It was, however, during this time that his interest in algebra broadened into quite a deep study of mathematics, including a very thorough investigation of calculus. When he entered Trinity College in 1810 he had a very full knowledge of mathematics.

Once at Cambridge he devoted most of his time to a study of the literature of mathematics, reading the works of the great mathematicians in their own languages and studying the French textbooks on calculus which were generally superior to the ones currently available in English. Babbage was so impressed by Lacroix's *Differential and Integral Calculus* that he formed a society along with John Herschel (later Sir John) and George Peacock, to translate the work into English and so modernise the teaching of calculus in the ancient universities.

The 'Analytical Society' as it was called, became much more important than this. Lacroix's book, along with the other continental works described the subject of differentiation in terms of $\frac{dy}{dx}$, which was largely unknown in England since the $\dot{x}$ notation of Newton was still in use. The continental notation came directly from the Leibniz branch of the discovery of the calculus, as has already been described. Babbage and his companions wished to replace Newton's dotage with Leibniz's d-ism. The Society, which was much scoffed at by professors and lecturers of the University, soon published a volume of transactions, written entirely by Herschel and Babbage, which was given the title of *The Principles of pure D-ism in opposition to the Dot-age of the University*. It is Babbage we have largely to thank for our now common $\frac{dy}{dx}$ notation in differential calculus. The Newtonian notation $\dot{x}$, $\ddot{x}$ . . . being reserved for $\frac{dx}{dt}$, $\frac{d^2x}{dt^2}$, ...

Life at Cambridge was not all serious mathematics. He liked to play chess, and did so with great skill. He spent time ghost hunting with other members of his ghost club, as has already been mentioned. He also liked sailing and from time to time he deviously obtained a spurious sickness certificate from a willing apothecary and embarked upon a nautical venture lasting several days.

In his final year at Cambridge, Babbage left Trinity College and took up residence at Peterhouse. The precise circumstances which caused this move have long been forgotten, but it is certain that he felt he was working in the mathematical shadow of Herschel and Peacock. Because of this he decided he would not suffer the ignominy of being placed third at Trinity. Instead, he took only a pass degree in 1814 but came first at Peterhouse. He then left Cambridge and went to live in London.

The following year the translation of Lacroix's book was published with the honours for the feat being equally divided between Babbage, Peacock and Herschel. The same year he published three papers on the calculus of functions; because of these attainments and his part in the translation, he was elected a Fellow of the Royal Society at the age of twenty-five.

Babbage's interest in calculating machines began one evening in Cambridge in 1812 while he was sitting in the rooms of his illustrious 'Analytical Society'. He was half asleep with a table of logarithms open at his side. Another member of the Society entered the room and called out to him, 'Well Babbage, what are you dreaming about?' He answered, 'I am thinking that all these tables might be calculated by machines'. This idea never really left him. While he worked on other aspects of mathematics, the need for such a machine seemed more and more obvious. Tables were laborious to prepare and were often so full of errors as to be at best of limited use and at worst dangerous. The nautical tables used on Royal Navy vessels of the time were so poor that navigators used captured French tables in their place; and it has been the case that unsuspecting enemy ships have been presented with the faulty British documents.

Babbage's childhood love of mechanisms was present in his dream of a calculating machine, but his desire to produce superior tables of all kinds was prominent. A machine once designed and operating, would neither tire nor make the kinds of mistakes that could be attributed to slips of the pen.

With his new wife Babbage toured Europe and learned a great deal about the construction of mathematical tables and, in particular, the ingenious division of labour used in this task by the French. On returning to England, he described his idea for a calculating engine to the distinguished scientist Wilfred Hyde Wollaston. This important pioneer of physics, metallurgy and chemistry encouraged Babbage to develop his ideas with the intention of building the machine.

Between 1820 and June 1822, Babbage built his first and only completed machine. It was intended as a prototype to explore and demonstrate the possibility of constructing mathematical tables using the method of differences. Before it can be briefly described, it is necessary to describe what is meant by the method of differences. This idea originated with Sir Thomas Harriot and was used almost immediately by Henry Briggs. Since that time this mathematical technique has been developed and used by many of the great mathematicians. If we take Babbage's own example $x^2 + x + 41$, and tabulate values for x:

x	$x^2 + x + 41$	D_1	D_2
1	43		
2	47	4	2
3	53	6	2
4	61	8	2
5	71	10	2
6	83	12	2
7	97	14	2
8	113	16	2
9	131	18	2
10	151	20	

The values in the column D_1, first order differences are calculated by subtracting values of $x^2 + x + 41$ obtained from consecutive values of x. E.g. 47 (x = 2) − 43 (x = 1) = 4. The values in column D_2, second order differences are obtained by subtracting consecutive values of D_1. All the second order differences are 2, a constant. (If we were to construct a third order difference column, it would contain only zeros.) Any quadratic expression, one containing terms in x^2, has constant second order differences. Also, any cubic expression, one containing terms in x^3, has constant third order differences. Indeed, any polynomial expression with terms of x^n, has constant nth order differences. This fact, together with a powerful mathematical theorem of Weierstrass, which states that any mathematical function can be approximated as a polynomial series, of the form $ax + bx^2 + cx^3 + \ldots + wx^n$, was of great importance in the theory behind Babbage's invention.

The whole idea behind Babbage's difference engine was that given the first values of a function, in this case 43, the first value of D_1 and the D_2, then the values of the function $x^2 + x + 41$ could be calculated by repetitive simple additions. As with 43 + 4 = 47, 47 + (4 + 2) = 53, 53 + (4 + 2 + 2) = 61, and so on. This, taken with the theorem of Weierstrass means that at least approximate tables of the important common functions such as logarithms, sines and cosines and tables of nautical information which can be described by a definite rule can be calculated in a simple but lengthy fashion.

Babbage's first machine was built to demonstrate that it was possible to perform the necessary additions by mechanical means. It worked only to the first two columns of differences but was capable of giving 6 to 8 figures. Right from the beginning it was intended that not only should tables be calculated mechanically, but that they should also be printed automatically, so that once the engine was set in motion, sheets of the completed tables were available without the intervention of the operator, and the possibility of transcription errors was eliminated. The completed 'Engine' worked well even though Babbage spent a large portion of his life experimenting with different printing methods. This first difference engine had pride of place in the Babbage home, and the inventor remained extremely proud of this creation for the rest of his life. At this point it should be pointed out that Babbage was not the sole inventor of the difference engine; thirty-five years earlier in 1786 one was proposed by J. H. Muller, but he was unable to put theory into practice and actually construct his machine. It is generally believed that Babbage never had any knowledge of this earlier idea.

Stimulated by his early success, Babbage set about building a new and more powerful difference engine. It was to be capable of working to sixth order differences, so it could deal with functions of the form $ax + bx^2 + cx^3 + dx^4 + ex^5 + fx^6$, and to handle numbers to twenty places of figures. But such an undertaking required a considerable sum of money to finance the experimentation, development and construction. Although Babbage was a man of considerable means (indeed, he inherited £40,000 from his father; a very large sum for the time) he sensibly wished the government to sponsor the machine, because they (mainly through the Royal Navy) and possibly scholars would be the principal beneficiaries; the machine would have no commercial value. His application was courteously received and a Committee of the Royal Society was set up to examine the request. Eventually they gave a favourable report and the government initially advanced the not inconsiderable sum of £1,500.

This new difference engine occupied most of his time. It could not simply be built as a scaled up version of his prototype. The drawings could not be completed without considerable experimental work. How would friction affect the engine's performance? How would the 'play' or backlash in the mechanism affect the machine's accuracy? In 1823, when

Babbage expected a relatively quick success, these appeared as only minor problems. However, he very soon had to hire a draughtsman for the production of drawings to a very high standard. Likewise, he sought the expertise of Joseph Clement, a highly skilled engineer with a workshop in Lambeth equal to any demands that engineers of the time could make. Soon the project tested the knowledge, abilities and patience of all those involved. Even Clement and his workmen were unequal to the task; new tools had to be made, new ways of working with metal devised and new standards of accuracy used. Joseph Whitworth (later Sir Joseph Whitworth, FRS) was one of Clement's workmen. He was destined to become one of the greatest engineers in an age of great engineers and probably one of the finest of all time. Whitworth, even from his youth, brought so many new methods of working and new standards of accuracy into his craft, that it could not be doubted that Babbage had the highest quality of workmanship involved in the construction of his engine. Yet progress was slow and expensive. Soon the original grant was overrun and the government was asked for more money. On the whole, the government matched its responsibility with cash. However, this was barely enough and Babbage spent much of his own money. Indeed, by about 1830, £7,000 had been consumed by the enterprise.

In the years since work had begun on the engine, Babbage had grown in scientific stature. When in 1826 the Lucasian Professorship of Mathematics at Cambridge fell vacant, he allowed his name to be given as a candidate for the position, even though he had never formally aspired to the highest mathematical honours of that or any other university. The other candidates were French and Airy, who later became Astronomer Royal; French, already ensconced in Cambridge as a college master, was elected. Babbage protested at this since French was a classicist. As the result, French resigned and Airy was elected. This was not the most flattering outcome so far as Babbage was concerned, but at least a very able mathematician was appointed to the chair once filled by Sir Isaac Newton. During Babbage's lifetime, considerable antipathy developed between him and Airy, whether or not it stemmed from this, I do not know, but Airy was no true supporter of Babbage or his computing enterprises. However, in 1828 Airy resigned in favour of accepting the chair of astronomy and the Lucasian chair was again vacant. Babbage's friends put his name forward and he was elected. During the period of the vacancy and the election he was touring Europe, and the first he heard of either his nomination or election was during his stay in Rome. His first reaction was to decline the invitation since he was deeply involved with the Difference Engine No. 1. However, his friends, and the delight he knew it would give his mother, caused him to reconsider. In the event he held the position until 1839, but he neither lived in Cambridge, nor did he give a single lecture. The only important part of his duties he took seriously was the assessment for and the award of the two Smiths' Prizes for the most able mathematics student within the University.

As the expense of the difference engine was beginning to get out of hand, Babbage sought a formal agreement with the government over funds. It was agreed after two years of haggling that the government would undertake formal responsibility for the cost. Babbage received the money he had spent out of his own pocket, outstanding bills were paid and it was agreed that part of the grounds of Babbage's house would be leased for the undertaking, and that extensive workshops would be built on this, adjoining his house. As the workshops were nearing completion in 1833, the part of the engine which had already been built was assembled. Babbage was very pleased with this, but further difficulties arose. Clement's workshops were in Lambeth, and his workshop had many more contracts than that for the difference engine, although this was certainly a substantial portion of the work. He was not very happy about the move to Babbage's workshops: he would have to split his workforce and would often be in the position of not having a suitable craftsman present in the right place for either Babbage's project or for the general work of his business. Clement demanded compensation and probably an improved rate of remuneration. To say the least, the whole enterprise was complicated, tedious and time-consuming. Clement wanted more money or to be rid of the contract. Babbage refused to pay what was demanded and Clement immediately stopped work and took his men and all the specially designed tools which had been made with him. These tools had been paid for from the government grants, but the law allowed him full possession. Clement even had the effrontery to offer to sell these to Babbage, but Babbage, having paid for them once was not about to do it a second time. At this time the cost involved was £17,000.

Babbage was now left in a state which could not have been pleasant. His work was not in ruins, but the possibility of finding someone else to take over where Clement had left off, with all the special skills, ideas and tools to be prepared or remade was remote. Yet Babbage did not give up. He was too involved in experimentation with the completed part of the engine.

Before we take the story further, it is important to describe a parallel event. In 1822, while Babbage was attempting to convince the Royal Society, initially through a letter to its president, Sir Humphry Davy, and the government of the worth of scientific and financial support for his idea, he published articles on the application of machines to the calculating of tables in the learned journals. However, it was not until 1834 that a lengthy article by another author, Dr Dionysius Larner, in the *Edinburgh Review* spread knowledge of his engine far and wide. This article was read by an enterprising, educated and wealthy printer, Pehr Georg **Scheutz** and his son Edvard. Apart from being a printer Scheutz was a lawyer and a scholar; he knew English well enough to translate the works of Scott and Shakespeare into Swedish. Scheutz was determined to try out the ideas of Babbage for himself. He sought Babbage's help with this and considerable encouragement was freely given. By 1843, the Scheutz had a small difference engine working. They tried to interest manufacturers in Sweden with their machine but no one saw it as having commercial potential. However, in 1851 Scheutz convinced the Swedish Academy of its usefulness to science and this body gave him a grant which allowed for a much larger and improved machine to be made. It worked to fifteen places of figures and used four orders of differences. A printing mechanism was incorporated and the whole machine worked very well, although its mechanism is dissimilar to that of Babbage's Engine. It was completed in 1853 and was immediately recognised as a triumph for engineering and science. The Great Paris Exhibition of 1855 awarded it a Gold Medal. Sweden honoured Scheutz with a knighthood and he received academic recognition by being accepted as a member of the Swedish Academy. The machine was exhibited throughout Europe, especially in London, before it was purchased for the Dudley Observatory at Albany, New York State by John F. Rathbone, a rich and scientifically enlightened benefactor.

This original machine worked in the Observatory for many years, producing astronomical tables and being involved with the tedious arithmetical work of the Observatory for three-quarters of a century. It was sold in 1924 and was sometime later acquired by the Smithsonian Institution. An exact copy of this machine was made by Messrs Bryan Donkin & Co. in 1859 for the British Government and it was used for the computation and printing of English life expectancy tables which were useful to insurance companies and government planners. For many years it was kept at Somerset House and was used by the Registrar General's staff. It is now in the Science Museum at South Kensington.

From Babbage's thinking and experiments in 1853, after Clement had abandoned work, came a new and wonderful idea. The output for the difference mechanism could be accumulated in a register and fed back into the engine in an appropriate way. Babbage called this feedback notion 'the engine eating its own tail'. This idea became not just a new means of extending the difference engine, but rather the seed for a new concept in calculating machines. From accumulating the output in a register came the whole new idea of a store. Not a passive store, but a dynamic one in which numbers could be stored, then withdrawn and operated upon and then stored again, together with the numbers generated in the calculations. Once this was possible then arithmetic could be done, not just once, but time and again: different numbers and different operations. Indeed, the idea was limitless, an engine could be built which would perform arithmetic and all that was needed were the numbers and the operation. This was the most difficult part of the theory; the engine needed instructions.

Babbage, having a natural affinity for all things mechanical, particularly those which used ingenious methods to great effect, was very familiar with the Jacquard device used on pattern weaving looms. Indeed, he possessed a woven picture of Jacquard himself made with the help of 24,000 Jacquard cards.

As we have seen, this was a considerable development in its own right, and Babbage was the first to apply this idea to computing machines. The punched cards of Jacquard were an obvious way to present information to a calculating engine. The arrangement of the punched holes was a coded store of information: numbers and instructions. Babbage realized almost immediately that these not only worked well in looms, but were also easy and cheap to prepare; they could be produced as the output of his new engine as well as be used as its input, and that they would develop into a permanent library. Once a set of instructions was punched onto cards, it could be used over and over again. Important numbers, such as logarithms or sines could be punched on to cards and fed into the machine whenever they were required. Along with the cards, Babbage intended to use barrels with pins attached to them, similar to those of barrel organs and musical boxes, for the transfer of mechanical information within his projected machine. He later reduced the number of these and increased the number of cards needed for the calculating process because of the ease of working with cards.

Babbage's idea for an analytical engine developed fast. He was soon at the stage where he required detailed drawings of the arithmetic unit and the storage devices. All his workmen had left with Clement, either to work on Clement's other projects or to take up lucrative employment in the building of railways, save one, his chief assistant. This man, who knew Babbage's ideas and how to set them out better than anyone, was set to follow the rest to a prosperous living with the railways, but he was enticed to stay by Babbage offering him payment of one guinea (£1.05) a day. This was an astronomical sum at the time and Babbage took advice from his mother before committing himself to paying it. His mother told him that if realising his ideas meant so much to him then he should pay what it cost, even if it meant living on bread and cheese.

By 1837, Babbage had progressed sufficiently to describe the concept of his analytical engine, what it could do and how it would work. There was even a detailed drawing of the important part of the mechanism (this was one of many which had been made in the light of experimentation) in the article which he wrote but it was never published during his lifetime. It describes how the calculating section of the engine was made up of two parts; the mill, where all the arithmetical operations were to be performed, and the store in which all the numbers were kept; numbers calculated by the machine were also kept there. Apart from the mill, made up from various mechanical carriages and barrels, Babbage considered the operation cards which told the engine which operations to perform and the 'combinatorial' cards which directed the combination of operations and the disposition of the various other cards within the engine to be the most important part of the mechanism. Some of the functions of the latter cards were later taken over by barrels. The store included the number cards and the 'Number Axis' which contained levers and wheels for registering as numbers the arrangement of holes in the cards. His description of the store also included various types of output devices. The results could be punched straight on to Jacquard-style cards, and, like his first difference engine, they could be printed. One step further than this was to have the engine punch the output figures directly on to copper plates. This permanent impression could be used at any time to recover a printed copy of the output; this was particularly useful for tables. It is, perhaps, worth remembering here that Babbage's motivation for all his work on calculating engines came from his desire to produce accurate tables which were free from misprints. He was not short of ideas for the output; reminiscent more of today's electronic computers than of Victorian mechanical wonders was his final idea for presenting the results of the analytical engine's machinations, a curve drawing apparatus. More cards, 'variable cards', were to control the operations of the store.

The engine was intended to perform addition, subtraction, multiplication, division and the extraction of roots to order, with numbers given to fifty figures and the store capable of retaining one thousand of these numbers. The whole machine was to be driven as an engine by a falling weight mechanism. This marvellous machine, which would certainly weigh several tons, was to work to the highest standards of precision (some of which were not then attainable), perform almost any useful piece of analytical arithmetic, and would truly have been one of the wonders of the mechanical world. The complexity of the task kept Babbage involved in attempting to produce designs for the mechanism until about 1846; he did not make any attempt to construct the machine. However, in 1840 he was invited to attend a scientific congress in Turin at the invitation of the Italian mathematician Giovanni Plana. At this meeting Babbage gave a lecture on the analytical engine which particularly interested L. F. Menabrea, then a talented army engineer (later to distinguish himself as a general). Babbage encouraged the young officer to write an account of his engine. This was published in Italian two years later.

This important published account would probably have sunk into obscurity if it had not been for one very able and determined lady, **Ada Augusta, Countess of Lovelace**. She was the only legitimate daughter of the poet Lord Byron. Lord and Lady Byron lived together for only a little over a year, and then separated forever one month after Ada was born. Byron never again saw his daughter, but they are buried together; she, like him, died in her thirties. Ada also seems to have inherited many of her famous father's talents. Her literary and linguistic talents were high, but it was in mathematics that she showed the greatest promise. Lady Byron encouraged her to pursue her interest in this subject. Amongst the friends of her mother were the De Morgans and the Somervilles. Augustus De Morgan, the famous mathematician who contributed to the theory of sets and Boolean algebra, took the young Miss Byron as a pupil. She became particularly adept and learned something of the higher reaches of the subject. Babbage was known by many of the great personages of science and mathematics including the De Morgans and Mrs De Morgan took Ada to visit him. She was much taken with his engines and where other visitors saw them as interesting curiosities beyond their understanding, Ada was immediately genuinely interested in and cognisant of their working. A friendship developed between Babbage and Miss Byron and her interest in his analytical engine was such that she undertook the translation into English of Menabrea's Italian account. She also added descriptive notes which were more than twice the length of the original article. This article was the best contemporary account of Babbage's analytical engine ever written. In 1835 Ada married Lord King, who eventually became the Earl of Lovelace.

To show the nature of the programming of the analytical engine we need to momentarily jump ahead to the work of

Babbage's youngest son, Major General H. P. Babbage, who, as we shall see, took a considerable interest in his father's machines. General Babbage gives in his own account, *The Analytical Engine* the following example of a program to compute: (ab + c)d.

Number card	Variable card	Operation card	
1			Places a on column 1 of Store
2			Places b on column 2 of Store
3			Places c on column 3 of Store
4			Places d on column 4 of Store
	1		Brings a from Store to Mill
	2		Brings b from Store to Mill
		1	Directs a x b = p
	3		Takes p to column 5 of Store
	4		Brings p into Mill
	5		Brings c into Mill
		2	Directs p + c = q
	6		Takes q to column 6 of Store
	7		Brings d into Mill
	8		Brings q into Mill
		3	Directs d x q = r
	9		Takes r to column 7 of Store
	10		Takes r to output (printer, card puncher, etc.)

In 1842 the British Government informed Babbage that it would no longer contribute towards the Difference Engine No. 1. This was purely the final announcement of what was already in effect, since progress on the machine had been suspended in 1833. However, four years later there was a change of government and Babbage once more returned to the subject of difference engines, hoping to incorporate that which he had learned in the planning of the analytical engine into a new attempt at building a large difference engine. It was not until 1857 that Babbage began serious work again on the analytical engine, this time beginning the actual construction of the machinery. Babbage had declined invitations to show his engines at the 1851 Crystal Palace Exhibition and the later one in Paris. In 1862 he did exhibit his inventions but the arrangements were such that a dark and out of the way position was given to him in the hall and they did not attract the attention they deserved. From then until his death fourteen years later he attempted what would have been one of the greatest engineering feats of the nineteenth century- to build the analytical engine. Years were, however, taken up in trying possible mechanisms, and in developing the tools that would shape steel and brass to the required tolerances. At the time of his death all that had been made, a few parts of the mill, was in pieces; his dream was unrealisable.

Babbage left all that existed of his engines, parts, drawings, tools and his workshop to his son. The General had to return to India in 1871, but three years later he returned and set about putting together part of the mill of the analytical engine. Expenses again proved heavy and H. P. Babbage had what remained of the new difference engine melted down; Babbage himself having previously used some of the pieces in his experiments with the analytical engine. With the help of assistants and workmen, General Babbage was able to complete the 1st to 44th multiples of π to 29 places of figures. Some mistakes were made and the General discontinued further experimentation except for a brief period in 1906 when he effected a repair to the faulty part of the mechanism. This machine, together with most of the other parts of Babbage's engines which have been constructed can now be seen in the Science Museum, South Kensington.

As has already been mentioned in this chapter, Babbage's life and work were paradoxical. He can be said to have devoted most of his adult life to his calculating engines, yet he wrote, invented and generally accomplished a great deal in many other fields of knowledge. Undoubtedly, his engines were frequently seen as failures, yet they are what he is remembered for; many of his other successes have come into the twentieth century as important parts of our life, yet they are far more subtle.

In the early years of the postal service, Babbage investigated the handling of mail and found that by far the greatest part of the cost was unrelated to the distance the letter or parcel was to be transported, but depended on the handling of the item. This discovery, an early piece of operational research, was influential in Sir Rowland Hill's introduction of the penny post.

Babbage also worked for a few months with the engineer Isambard Kingdom Brunel on the Great Western Railway.

He investigated the power and motion of railway locomotives and their trains and developed an early dynamometer car. The occulting light, shone to mariners from lighthouses, was also of his design. As a spin-off from the work on his engines he invented new tools and methods and considerably aided the progress of mechanical engineering. In the course of this work he devised a notation and calculus for describing the operations of machinery. His other interests included locksmithing and deciphering coded messages.

There were also some less well-conceived projects. With Lady Lovelace he devised a scheme for making money by betting on the horses. But like all other attempts at racing systems, it did not work. Horses were neither as consistent nor as logical as the mathematics they were supposed to obey! Instead of making money to aid the production of his engines, the enterprise caused a near financial disaster for both Babbage and Ada. Babbage's fascination with mechanical devices was also shown in his plan to make a machine to play noughts and crosses; the winnings from this enterprise were also to go towards his engines. Another ill-founded scheme for the same purpose was to write a long, three-volume novel. It was to realise £5,000, but in the end it too came to nothing.

That this novel was abandoned was not because of his lack of literary skills; Babbage was an accomplished and influential writer on philosophical and scientific topics. As we have seen, his early works were mathematical. Later there was also an extensive table of logarithms, published by the Hungarian Academy of Sciences and tables of other mathematical functions. In his book *Economy of Machinery and Manufacture* he analysed the division of labour in production processes and contributed towards the founding of operational research.

One of Babbage's philosophical and theological writings began in a negative sense with the bequest of £10,000 by the Earl of Bridgewater in 1829 to write books 'on the Power, Wisdom and Goodness of God as manifested in the Creation'. Eight authors were commissioned for these Bridgewater treatises by a committee composed of the President of the Royal Society and a number of bishops. Babbage was not selected, so, not to be outdone, he wrote his own *The Ninth Bridgewater Treatise*. This was far superior to all of the others. Amongst its wisdom is Babbage's conception of God as a kind of programmer, with which he explains miracles as the Creator's program by which out of character results are computed by design after very long intervals in which only simple expected results occur. It is a similar process to that of one of his own engines printing two thousand natural numbers, then a square number, then another long sequence of natural numbers, followed by another novel result.

During the later 1820s he became concerned about the decline of science. He placed much of the blame for this on the Royal Society in general and Sir Humphry Davy in particular, even though this great man was not then alive to defend himself. In a recent election of the President of the Society, a wealthy landowner had been chosen and not a worthy scientist. To make his views known to a wide audience, he embodied them in his very influential book *Reflections on the Decline of Science* published in 1830. This book, and an article by Sir David Brewster, contributed directly to the formation of the British Association for the Advancement of Science at York in 1831. This new society was an open alternative to the Royal Society and it was modelled on the German Society, Deutsches Naturforschers Versammlung, with which Babbage had become acquainted on his many continental visits. Babbage also played a leading role in the formation of the Royal Astronomical Society in 1820 and the Royal Statistical Society in 1834.

During the earlier part of his life, before he became obsessed with his calculating engines, Babbage mixed with the elite of European society. He was welcomed by scientists, writers, philosophers, statesmen and many other influential people. Many were entertained in his home on their visits to England. As his life passed, he sought seclusion, and his machines dominated his life. The sparkle and intelligence he used to show in conversation deteriorated in later life to the extent that even his best and longest standing friends had great difficulty in understanding him. He attempted to find peace in which to think and work, but in this he mishandled things. The hustle and bustle of London, with its street sounds annoyed him. In particular, the organ grinders, which were fairly common, disturbed him. This raucous music caused him to attempt to direct them away from his home by all the official means he could muster. The result, of course, was the very reverse. Like unruly children who will taunt their teacher when they learn they can annoy him without incurring an effective deterrent, the street musicians of all kinds came singly and in bands miles out of their way just to torment Babbage. When he left his home to go about his business in London, processions of people would follow him, baiting him with their cackle and deafening him with their brand of music making, while young children pelted him with mud and horse dung from the roads.

The great mechanical philosopher, perhaps, did not notice these cruel indignities, for he was inventing the computer. That he failed to create his mechanical dreams was his fault only in that he underestimated the task. It was not until Howard Aiken built the massive electro-mechanical Harvard Mark 1 Computer in the early 1940s that Babbage's dream was realised.

Despite all the set-backs and irritations, Charles Babbage lived to the ripe old age of eighty, dying in London on the 18th October 1871.

CHAPTER SIX

Herman Hollerith

BABBAGE'S ENGINES were very definitely machines intended to aid the mathematician, astronomer or scientist. They were for finding the answers to very definite problems, even if this involved the construction of tables. Modern computers usually do not perform this function at all. They are involved with processing payrolls, keeping accounts or controlling the stock of a factory. In fact, one important area of computer development has involved the capacity to count and marshal large amounts of data, without performing anything much more mathematical than simple addition and subtraction.

Throughout the nineteenth century there was a vast increase in the amount of all kinds of accounting. The quantity of paper work being carried out rose from very little at the beginning of the century to a gigantic amount at the end, requiring whole armies of clerks and officials. It was during this time that nations became concerned with their populations and rates of development. Large surveys were carried out and a general move throughout Europe and the USA was made to improve social conditions, employment, education and health. While information had been gathered and simple statistics prepared in many nations for thousands of years, the need and desire to count and classify reached a point never before envisaged. The growth of rail transport and the spread of mass-produced goods also heralded a need for counting which had previously been unknown.

Censuses in which people were simply counted began to be held by law in Britain and the USA. These were lengthy processes, although not unduly complicated at first. As the

Herman Hollerith. (Photo: *Science Museum, London.*)

century progressed there were vast changes in population. For instance, between 1880 and 1890 the population of the USA increased by over 20 per cent. Also the movement towards better living conditions meant that more knowledge was needed about the people. To count heads was simply not enough; there was also a need to collect statistics on industrial and agricultural production, on the use of energy, the amount of building and the development of transportation networks. 'Statistics' was an appropriate name, for the gathering of information about the 'state'.

It is not surprising that the people who handled the vast quantities of information should feel that they were fighting a losing battle. Every census or survey required more work and took far longer than the previous one. It was not uncommon to be planning or even carrying out a survey before the results of the previous one were processed. Many clerks and organisers must have wondered whether there was an easier way, but have been too busy or too involved with the job in hand to do anything about it. That eventually one person was not was fortunate for both the information gatherers and the development of the computer. The tenth US Census in 1880 coped with the details of 50,000,000 people; and it took seven and a half years to tabulate the information, but out of this mammoth task developed the embryo of the Hollerith Electric Tabulating System.

Herman **Hollerith** was born in Buffalo, New York on the 29th February 1860. His parents had left Germany only twelve years earlier because of the political disturbances. In fact, the Hollerith family was just one more group of people in the massive influx into the USA which caused the census figures to increase so rapidly. The Holleriths had come to America to give their children something which they could not get in Europe; a good education. Herman is said to have been a bright and able child at school, but had an inability to learn spelling easily. His determined teacher made his life miserable to the extent that he used to avoid school whenever possible and run away when his teacher showed renewed effort to improve his spelling. Eventually he was removed from school and received private lessons from the Lutheran minister whose church the family attended. Herman's progress was such that he was soon able to enter the School of Mines of Columbia

University. He graduated with an engineering degree in 1879, aged twenty.

He had been a very able student and had attracted the attention of one of his teachers, Professor William P. Trowbridge. This was perhaps the first of a fortunate set of circumstances which was to benefit Hollerith personally and eventually the US censuses and data processing generally. Herman was made Trowbridge's assistant, and later Trowbridge was appointed a Chief Special Agent to the Census Office. This brought young Hollerith into the work of the 1880 Census.

His main task was not to deal with the people at all, but to examine statistics related to the manufacturing industry. In this he could use his knowledge of engineering, but he must have been aware of the handling of vast quantities of raw data going on all round him. He carried his own task to a very satisfactory end by producing the *Report on Power and Machinery Employed in Manufactures*, published by the Census Office in 1888.

In charge of the section of the Census dealing with the statistics related to the people and dealing with life and death (vital statistics) was Dr. John Shaw Billings. As has been mentioned earlier, the ten-yearly census increased in size and organisation from one decade to the next. Billings was a surgeon, a Major, in the US Army, and had been drafted to help the organisation of work in 1870. He had shown considerable interest and organising ability in 1870 and had been sent for again in 1880, this time as senior adviser. That Billings played an important role in data processing, we shall see later, but his work with the censuses was only part of this remarkable man's achievements. He rose to the position of Deputy Surgeon General and as a long-serving expert on public health and vital statistics, he became professor of hygiene at the University of Pennylvania on his retirement. Two years later he left to turn the New York Public Library, one of the finest libraries in the world, into its present form.

Often when we have a good idea, it appears so obvious that we wonder why we have taken so long to arrive at it; also, we often think that if we have found it then it must be obvious to everyone else. Good ideas are frequently very simple, yet they take a long time to stand naked in the mind in their stark simplicity. Two or three fortunate encounters with the nebulous idea are sometimes needed before its importance is realised. Because of this there are often several authentic stories about a discovery, all in some respect true. This would seem to be the case in this instance. But the precise order in which the fruitful encounters occurred is only to be guessed at.

One story of the genesis of the idea comes from Walter W. Wilcox, who contributed to a history of the use of punched cards in the US Censuses. He relates that Hollerith had told him that one day Billings was walking through the large office, where hundreds of clerks were working at transferring data from the returns of the enumerators, in the company of Hollerith. Billings is reputed to have said, 'There ought to be some mechanical way of doing this job, something on the principle of the Jacquard loom, whereby holes in a card regulate the pattern to be woven'. No doubt Billings was fully aware of the engineering knowledge of his companion.

Another story comes from a letter which Hollerith wrote. Here Hollerith describes that he had tea with Dr Billings and his family one Sunday evening and Billings said that he thought there should be a machine for carrying out the routine tasks of tallying. Some discussion on the possibilities then ensued.

What follows in both accounts is that Hollerith asked Billings if he wanted to work with him and have a share in his developments. Billings declined this and Hollerith went on to develop his system on his own. The origin of the idea to use the Jacquard loom principle lay plainly with Billings but all the rest was Hollerith's.

In 1882, when his part of the census work was complete, Hollerith accepted a position as instructor in mechanical engineering at the Massachusetts Institute of Technology (MIT). During the short period he spent as teacher and academic engineer, he examined the mechanism of the Jacquard device for pattern weaving and came to two conclusions. One was that Jacquards were very different in function to what was required to count a census, the other was that Jacquard cards were very efficient stores of information. He believed that there was certainly an important idea in Billing's suggestion, but there was need for further thought and an overall idea of how the counting would work from beginning to end.

One night he was travelling by train, and in between moments of dozing he heard the conductor punching tickets. How long this had gone on that night, and how many times before he had heard the same sound and seen the same task being performed, he did not know – it was common place. But in this simple and ubiquitous task he realised how the holes were to get into the Jacquard cards; they were to be punched in by a conductor's punch.

Hollerith's early experiments at MIT began simply. He thought a whole card carrying as much information as that for a Jacquard would be difficult to handle, so his first machine used paper tape. The holes were punched into the tape with a hand punch, and as the tape went over a drum electrical contacts were made through the holes in the tape and counters were activated. Electricity being conducted had taken the place of Jacquard's needles. These ideas of punched holes and electrical contacts were good and sound but the rest of the machine had drawbacks. The tape had to be still to count the holes, so the great advantage of the paper strip was lost. There could be no continuous running and the efficiency of the counting was based on the speed of action of the mechanism which would stop the tape, place the electrical contacts in position, count the electrical impulses and then move the tape forward to the next set of holes. The speeding up of this process was an engineering problem and could eventually be improved. The real problem was the same as that which Bouchon had faced with his loom; the paper tape did not carry enough information. Relatively rare pieces of information would be miles apart in the tape, and the tape, unlike cards, could not be sorted. Hollerith applied for patents for these devices in 1884, but he knew that something better was needed. Consequently, he allowed the applications to lapse, but when he refiled for patents they were based on his much improved card system.

In the meantime he discovered that the job of university teacher was not for him, and although he did not want to disappoint General Francis Waller, a friend from his work in the 1880 Census who, on appointment as President of MIT had persuaded him to take the academic job he offered, he left for work in St. Louis. St. Louis was a change, not from inventing, just from punched cards. During the next year he worked as a railway engineer and experimented with braking systems, particularly electro-mechanically operated air brakes. Although this work interested and stimulated him it absorbed too much of his attention. He wanted to be working on his punched card machines.

Whether he made his next move by design or whether it was purely good fortune, circumstances were in his favour; he gained a position with the Patent Office in Washington in 1884. This gave him both the opportunity to learn the ins and outs of patenting and have easy access to the literature describing thousands of patents and to spend very much more time developing his machines. It was during this period, which lasted until 1890, that the Hollerith Electric Tabulating System came into being.

As he developed his ideas, he needed data on which to test them. One of his first large scale counting exercises concerned surveys from the City of Baltimore in 1887. Here he rejected the paper strip and used stout cards $8\frac{5}{8}$ inches long by $3\frac{1}{4}$ inches wide. Hollerith recorded each death that occurred in the town by punching a hole with a conductor's punch, the actual application of the idea which came to him on the train journey. Each card had three rows of spaces at the top, three at the bottom and some at one end. Hollerith treated the cards rather like train tickets and punched around the rows; his punch would not reach further into the ticket than the three rows and so his cards were not fully utilised.

The last five years of the 1890s was a period of intense activity for Hollerith. The development and construction of his machines took place at a rapid pace. Engineering improvements were obvious as soon as his initial crude machines were being made. He became involved in the processing of certain data, particularly for small departments of the US Government and civil and military medical services. As well as his desire to shorten the length of time spent on machines, he was concerned about the cards he used. It was easy to treat cards as tickets and design them so that they recorded well-identified categories, like deaths in Baltimore. His design of special purpose cards was important. One which he made up during his career concerned sickness in the US Army. It identified with punched holes the man, his rank and unit, the nature of his illness and the number of days he was unfit for duty together with consequent alterations in his pay. Special punches soon replaced the crude ticket punch. As far as cards were concerned, he soon realised that what was required was a small, easily handled pattern which could contain a lot of information, yet withstand punching and hand and machine handling.

The next US Census occurred in 1890. The authorities realised that there would be an enormous amount of data to be digested but they were aware that a number of engineers and inventors were working on a mechanised handling process. As the time of the Census neared, a committee was set up by the Superintendent of the Census, Robert P. Porter. In 1889 this body invited the submission of data processing systems for the Eleventh US Census. Hollerith's system was already known to work well, but there were others. The committee contained John Billings, so there was definite support for Hollerith's system. Another member of the judging body was William C. Hunt. He managed to act for both sides, since he had a tabulating system of his own. As well as the two systems mentioned, there was a third, belonging to Charles F. Pidgin.

The test for the systems was to be a comprehensive one. Returns from the already processed 1880 Census from four districts of the city of St. Louis were recounted and tabulated by each of the three competitiors. For the count the Hollerith system took 72 hours and 27 minutes, while its nearest rival, the Pidgin system took 110 hours and 56 minutes, and Hunt's took 144 hours and 25 minutes (almost exactly twice as long as the winner). For tabulating the returns as useful and ordered information, the Hollerith system took 5 hours and 28 minutes, a very decisive victory over the 44 hours and 41 minutes taken by Pidgin and 55 hours and 22 minutes taken by Hunt. Hollerith clearly demonstrated the superiority of his apparatus and method. It was estimated that approximately 65,000,000 people were living in the USA and that a very conservative estimate of the saving to the Census authorities of $600,000 would be made if Hollerith's machines were used rather than the previous methods. Consequently, Hollerith was awarded the contract to process the Census data.

This was only the beginning. Before the work could start, many preparations had to be made. Hollerith engaged the Pratt and Whitney Company (later famous for its aero engines) to construct the punches. These were keyboard punches, which could be used rather like a simple and crude typewriter. The counting apparatus was built by the Western Electric Company. All was ready by 1st June 1890. As the returns began to come in during the middle of September, the machines and their operators set to work. The cards were punched at a rate far greater than was expected. All went so well, that a rough count of the population was available before the last returns reached the Census office. On the 12th December, the full count was known, 62,622,250. This of course, did not include the vast number of statistical tabulations and analyses which were probably the most important part of the Census. The Hollerith machines were very superior in this task and again, in record time, such tabulations as were required became available. The evaluation and analytical reports that follow in the wake of the counting and tabulations took a relatively longer time.

The Hollerith tabulating system allowed more categories of information to be collected and processed than ever before, and it was instrumental in extending the Census aims further than had ever before been considered practicable. For the first time the US Government was able to accurately ascertain: the number of children born in a family, the number of children still alive in a family and the number of members of a family who spoke English.

Hollerith submitted his work on tabulating systems for a doctorate in philosophy, which was awarded by the Columbia School of Mines in 1890. His thesis described the system in all its elegant detail. The cards used were $3\frac{1}{4}$ inches by $6\frac{5}{8}$ inches (the same size as a dollar bill) and had 288 positions to receive punch holes. These comprised 240 positions in 10 rows of 24 in the main body of the card and 2 additional rows at the top of the card for further coded information. A corner was cut off each of the manila cards to indicate the correct way it should be placed in the punch. Often, many cards were punched at once and heavy duty gang punches were used which were capable of punching a hole in any combination of the 240 positions in the main body of the cards. Even before the cards were transferred to the counting apparatus, certain checks were made by pushing wire needles through appropriate holes in packs of the cards to discover mistakes. This techniques was also used to discover relatively rare characteristics.

For counting, the cards were transferred one at a time to a kind of gang punch in reverse. A press containing 240 needles was pulled down onto each card individually, those needles which struck unpunched cards were pressed back on their springs while those which encountered holes carried on through the card and met electrical contacts (each filled with mercury to ensure good conduction). The electric circuits which the needles completed activated counters. Hence, each hole was counted with the use of electricity. In practice, the cards were counted quickly and as the counters had one hundred divisions they were capable of counting 100×100 holes (10,000) without being reset. Although the cards were passed through the machine quickly, a bell was arranged to ring when electrical contact had been made, so that if a card had been improperly punched no bell would sound and it could be removed for detailed examination.

The tabulating section of the system was, for the time, very novel. The operator arranged electrical connections so that when a card possessing any information which he was interested in was discovered a circuit would be activated. These circuits opened doors in a battery of 24 small boxes. As the press passed through the holes indicating the required combination of information, the door of the appropriate box opened electrically. The operator then placed the card in the box and closed it by hand. The great advantage was that quite complex combinations could be wired up to open a door. Even by hand, the card could be handled quickly and so important and rare sets of information could be found and tabulated quickly. The actual written tabulation was carried out by a clerk, but all the required data was present in the piles of cards which he took from the boxes of the tabulator.

The system proved to be so efficient that the still extensive handling of individual cards was not seen as a great disadvantage. This was later to contribute to the downfall of the Hollerith system, since others saw ways to automate the process and to incorporate a printer, thus doing away with much of the clerical assistance which had been required.

In 1889 Hollerith had taken out patents covering his machines and so during the 1890s he enjoyed considerable success, financial and otherwise. Honours and recognition flowed quickly in his direction. The prestigeous Franklin Institute of Philadelphia gave him their highest award, the Elliott Cresson medal in 1890. He was awarded a gold medal at the Great Paris Exposition, and he received a Bronze Medal from the 1893 World's Fair. Also he was held in high academic esteem, lecturing to such learned bodies as the Royal Statistical Society, London.

Economic prosperity came his way when census bodies throughout the world requested the use of his system and called upon his personal expertise. During 1891 alone, his machines were used in Canada, Norway and Austria. The more far-sighted captains of industry and commerce also showed an interest in data handling techniques. In response to this he adapted existing machines and designed others to handle first the accounts and statistics of the New York Central and Long Island railroads, then the accounts of other railways. Soon manufacturing and retailing companies sought his advice and machines for handling their payrolls, credits and stock control procedures. Within a few years he had adapted, designed and built punched card systems that quickly and effectively carried out the paperwork of many types of businesses. Indeed, it was during this decade that the punched card office came into being, even though it was during the first quarter of the twentieth century that it became both automatic and commonplace. Everything went so well for Hollerith that in 1896 he organised the Tabulating Machine Company, which he based in New York, to produce his machines and develop his business systems. The shortcoming of some of his devices had been realised, and by automating the handling of the cards, great savings were made in the operation.

For the Twelfth US Census in 1900, Hollerith's machines were hired. Certainly the US Government paid a high price for the privilege of an automated count and tabulation of its returns, and this high price was noted. Part of the expense was caused by the techniques used to handle agricultural statistics, which required a different treatment to the population data. An estimate was made which showed that a traditional clerical operation could have accomplished the task more cheaply, but certainly not in such a short time.

When, in 1903, Congress passed the Permanent Census Bureau Act, making the Census Bureau a permanent body, the first director, S. N. D. North, investigated the matter. The result was that a section was set up within the Bureau to develop data processing equipment. Even though this section had sizeable funds, it was not certain that they would have enough time to prepare their own machines for the 1910 Census. However, during the next few years their developmental laboratory made a significant improvement in punched card machines. They made their own version of the Hollerith system by skirting around the Hollerith patents, but instead of the electrical 10,000 unit counters, they developed an automatic printing device. These machines had been built under the direction of their engineer James Powers and were ready in principle by 1907. Powers was one of the most fortunate inventors in history since he persuaded the Census Bureau to allow him to personally hold the patents to the machines.

Hollerith had, all along, hoped that the Bureau's development activities would fail to mature in time for the 1910 Census so that he would still get the lucrative contract. It was not to be; he returned from a trip to Europe and Russia where he had been acting as a consultant and contractor for several censuses and business enterprises, to find that he would not be required to provide his machines and services for the Thirteenth US Census.

In 1911 Powers, replete with patents, left the Bureau and set up his own firm, The Powers Tabulating Machine Company. Almost immediately, it became a powerful competitior against Hollerith's Tabulating Machine Company. Powers had the advantage of manufacturing machines based on designs which had benefited from Hollerith's experience. It was not long, therefore, before Hollerith's company not only lost its total market outlet domination but was seen as a fairly poor second best. When, in 1911, the Tabulating Machine Company amalgamated with the Computing Scale Company of America and Time Recording Company of New York, the benefits of the merger disappeared very quickly, leaving the new Computing-Tabulating-Recording Company to make most of its profit from time clocks and weighing machines.

Hollerith's role in the new company was that of engineer. The regeneration of the firm largely came about through the determination and organisational skills of one man, Thomas J. Watson. Watson was not an engineer, he was a man who had learned business from the bottom. His early experience as a salesman and agent working in rural areas of the United States gave him confidence in his supreme abilities.

He joined the Computing-Tabulating-Recording Company in 1918 and within three months he became its president. There followed considerable reorganisation so that by 1920 the business had recovered its lost ground and gained sufficient orders and credibility to carry it through the hard economic times which America was facing. In 1924 the company was renamed International Business Machines (IBM). Further integration of IBM's structure took place in 1933, and from then the company developed into the giant organisation it is today with a superlative reputation in the field of digital computers and a very substantial share of the world market.

The Power's company also went through considerable evolution. In 1927 it merged with the Remington-Rand Corporation to become its Tabulating Machines Divisions. Later, in 1955 Remington-Rand amalgamated with Sperry Gyroscope to make the Sperry-Rand Corporation.

The rival Powers and Hollerith Companies dominated the manufacture of punched card machines and the supply of office machines in the United States and through much of the rest of the world, including England, until after the end of the Second World War, when electronic computers began to be developed. Although large-scale punched card systems had neither the efficiency nor the power of modern systems and they did not pervade business and government to the same extent, they were very important to the whole sphere of commerce and they were truly the crude forerunners of modern data processing machines.

Herman Hollerith stayed with the Computing-Tabulating-Recording Company as consultant engineer until his retirement in 1921. Even during his retirement he considered ways of improving his data handling machines. However, he was not to enjoy his retirement for long. On the 17th November 1929 he died in Washington DC from a heart attack. He had given the censuses and worlds of statistics and commerce a way of improving the Jacquard card and using it to hold, transfer, count and tabulate information. Such cards are sometimes still known as Hollerith cards but now they have 80 or 96 columns instead of his 24. Also the code for entering information on to cards is known as the Hollerith code. His name is still remembered in the H for Hollerith format in the Fortran programming language. Paper tape, the use of which he discarded, has also been used as an important medium for feeding information into the computer.

CHAPTER SEVEN

Vannevar Bush

AS IN THE development of life on earth, the evolution of the computer produced a race of dinosaurs which grew from small beginnings into a number of huge complex structures which flourished briefly and then disappeared forever; only now to be seen mutilated and disembodied as curiosities in the corners of museums.

Up to now the machines we have described have been concerned with the ordinary processes of arithmetic and counting, sometimes on a large scale. For the businessman and the statistician this is enough, speed and quantity are his concerns. The scientist and engineer have scarcely benefited because their concerns are as much with the operations of mathematics as with those of arithmetic. Much of the information concerned with the world about us and with the design and operation of machines is available in expressions which indicate how one quantity varies with another; and not uncommonly in the form of how a particular quantity varies with time. Physics, chemistry, biology, economics and electrical, mechanical and civil engineering are riddled with problems expressed in this form. The solution of these depends on explicitly finding something which can be found experimentally only as a rate of variation. In such mathematical processes the calculus is involved.

Fortunately, the expression of the variation of y and x by derivatives of the form $\frac{dy}{dx}$, $\frac{d^2y}{dx^2}$ etc. can in principle be evaluated by integration.

Vannevar Bush with the Product Integraph. (Photo: *The Smithsonian Institution*.)

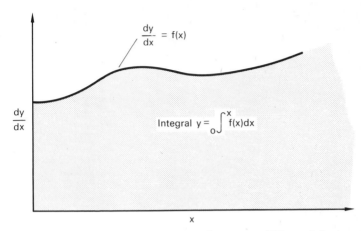

$$\frac{dy}{dx} = f(x)$$

$$\text{Integral } y = \int_0^x f(x)dx$$

$$\frac{dy}{dx}$$

$$\frac{dy}{dx}$$

x

Equations involving derivatives are known as differential equations. For example,

$$\frac{dy}{dx} = xy, \quad \frac{d^2y}{dx^2} = -n^2y, \quad \left(\frac{d^2y}{dx^2}\right)^2 + 3xy\frac{dy}{dx} = x^2y$$

are equations of this type. Integration can be considered as the converse of differentiation, the process of finding a derivative and hence it can be used to find y from $\frac{dy}{dx}$. Also it can be considered to be the area between the curve $\frac{dy}{dx} = f(x)$ and the x-axis in a suitable graph.

The solution of differential equations is part of the activity of engineers and scientists. However, not all the equations that turn up are amenable to solution. By the ordinary methods of mathematics only certain classes of them can be solved. Others can be solved, but their solutions given in closed form cannot be easily handled to achieve numerical answers. Probably most equations are plainly unsolvable by what we usually consider to be ordinary mathematics. In short, the time and bother which these ubiquitous and difficult things cause is a serious nuisance to those who would rather be in the laboratory, drawing office or workshop. Because of this, engineers and scientists, rather than mathematicians, have attempted to find ways of creating some analogy or physical model of integration. In its simplest form this is not entirely a difficult task. Methods of calculating areas have been used for centuries, and accurate instruments (planimeters) for this purpose were developed at the beginning of the nineteenth century and are still in common use with land surveyors and estate agents. The scientist however, requires something which is both highly adaptable and accurate to within a few per cent.

The first indication of an integrator suitable for the solution of differential equations came from the renowned Scottish physicist, James Clerk **Maxwell** in 1855. Maxwell was born in 1831 in Edinburgh. He did not distinguish himself during his early school days, but his intellectual faculties developed during his teens. It was at Edinburgh University that he began his higher education, but he went on to Trinity College, Cambridge three years later in 1850. After graduating with high honours in mathematics he became a fellow of his college. He was appointed to professorships of natural philosophy, what we would now call physics, at Aberdeen and later at King's College, London. He came out of retirement from his estates in Scotland to become the first Cavendish Professor of Experimental Philosophy at Cambridge in 1871. Once there he was responsible for the design of the Cavendish Laboratory. At about this time, 1873, he published his famous work *Treatise on Electricity and Magnetism* which explained the electrical and magnetic phenomena that had already been observed in terms of the famous Maxwell Equations. This treatise has formed the basis of modern thinking on the subject. Six years after this triumph, Maxwell died in Cambridge in 1879.

Maxwell never constructed his integrator but the principle was sound. A disc was rotated by a shaft A. On the disc was a small wheel B, attached to another shaft C. As the disc rotated so would the wheel B; the amount of rotation would depend on the distance of the wheel from the centre of the disc.

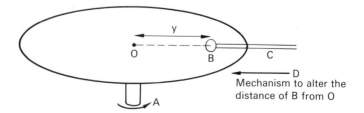

Mechanism to alter the distance of B from O

If the rotation of the shaft A expressed the quantity x and the distance of the wheel B from the centre O of the disc expressed the quantity y then the output rotation of shaft C expressed the quantity $\int y dx$. Hence the angle turned by C represented the integration of the distance y with respect to the angle turned by A. Of course y and x are variables and the value of y will depend on x, and so for a uniformly increasing x the distance y will vary. Sometimes y will be close to 0, other times it will be far away; it is quite possible for y to pass to the opposite side of the disc and represent $-y$, a negative quantity. A mechanism for altering the position of B was also needed. This idea of a mechancial analogy of integration was not taken up for some time and then not in practical terms.

It was another equally famous physicist, Lord **Kelvin** (William Thomson) renowned for his contribution to the theory of electricity, who made the next small but significant step. Kelvin, unlike Maxwell, showed his intellectual powers early; he entered the University of Glasgow at the age of ten. Later he went on to Peterhouse, Cambridge and attained almost identical honours to Maxwell. Although he was elected a Fellow of Peterhouse shortly after his graduation in 1846, he took up the position of Professor of Natural Philosophy at Glasgow almost immediately. Kelvin was knighted in 1866 for his contribution to the laying of the first Transatlantic Cable. In 1892 he was made a peer and he died in 1907. Although famous for his contribution to electricity and thermodynamics, and the study of heat and work, he constructed a number of integrators. His most ambitious machines were for calculations concerned with the prediction of tides and the analysis of the mathematical components which govern their nature. Kelvin's brother James, a professor of engineering at Belfast and then Glasgow, devised part of the mechanism used in these instruments and constructed the first integrator based on Maxwell's idea during the 1860s. For our purpose, however, Kelvin's contribution was to show in principle that two of Maxwell's integrators suitably coupled together could be used to solve second order differential equations.

Equations of this kind involve second derivatives (of the form $\frac{d^2y}{dx^2}$), and are one of the most common types of differential equations encountered by scientists. One of the reasons for this is that they are deeply involved with Newton's equations and Newton's Second Law of Motion in Mechanics. To have a device to solve equations of this type would clearly be an advantage to the world of science. Unfortunately there were problems. The output, shaft C, of the first integration would need to become the input, shaft A, of the second integrator and B would never possess enough torque, or turning force, to set this shaft in motion. There was no obvious way to solve this problem, but Kelvin's idea remained. The difficult differential equations remained, a stimulus to anyone with the ability to construct a computer to solve them. It was, again, a man whose scientific work had been involved with electricity who took up the challenge. In principle, Kelvin showed how integrators could be coupled together in various ways to trick difficult equations into submission; indeed, he outlined a computer which could handle differential equations of the nth order using n integrators. These ideas lay fallow for half a century until a new stimulus was given in the form of difficult equations stemming from the development of electrical theory by Vannevar Bush.

Bush was one of the greatest members of the American scientific scene during the twentieth century. He was a man of boundless energy and was successful as an inventor, scientist, engineer, organiser and administrator at the highest level and as such he became one of the elder statesmen of the scientific establishment in the United States.

Vannevar **Bush** was born in 1890 in Everett, Massachusetts, which is a little to be north of Boston. His ancestors had been fishermen and so at first was his father, Richard Perry Bush, but he left this occupation with a determination to gain a college education. After he succeeded in this, he became a clergyman and devoted the rest of his life to the church. It was in an atmosphere of activity, strict religious observance and determination that Vannevar grew up. During his childhood he suffered from typhoid and rheumatic fevers. The prolonged confinement to the home which these caused directed his energy towards investigating and manipulating the things around him. He experimented with radio at a time when this was a new and highly novel activity. All things mechanical and electrical attracted him. It seemed natural that he would become an engineer, and so it was that he went to Tuft's College, like his father, to study engineering. He had no time to be lazy or to live in an ivory tower; his family were short of money and there were no grants, so Vannever had to work his way through college. To his rescue came his ability to organise, which was to remain with him throughout his life. After a period of washing dishes, he discovered people would pay to be taught mathematics, so he organised his first few students to find and advertise his lessons to others. Soon he had a flourishing enterprise in progress.

In 1913, at the age of twenty-three, Bush graduated. During his student days he had contrived to invent new devices, learning the practical tricks of the workshop and the technique of transforming an idea into reality. Some of his ideas made more useful and successful machines than others, but at almost the same time as he obtained his bachelor's degree he produced his first really important invention. This was a machine with which to survey land and produce a profile of its rise and fall with horizontal distance travelled. The mechanism was housed between two bicycle wheels. The movement of the wheels transmitted the motion of the machine to a disc to whcih were connected two rollers; one of these recorded the vertical distance travelled while the other operated a paper roll on which was recorded the horizontal distance. Bush's machine was not unlike a large Maxwell-Thomson integrator, and it was with this that he met for the first time many of the problems of design which he later found with his computers. Apart from the actual integrator it contained an automatically winding spring, which served as a continuous energy store and a feedback device known as a servomechanism. Academically, the 'surveyor' was a success, he was awarded a master's degree for the project shortly after his initial graduation. But, although he was awarded a patent for it, it was not a potential money-maker and was never manufactured commercially.

Bush left Tuft's College and began work for the General Electric Company but this proved to be a mistake. His salary was very low, the job was little more than menial and he was made redundant after a fire had temporarily reduced the amount of work for the depot where he worked. Fortunately at this time, a junior lectureship became vacant at his old college. Shortly after taking up this post he set about the study and research necessary for a doctorate in engineering. Characteristic of his efforts in all things, he obtained the D. Eng. degree, which was awarded jointly by the Massachusetts Institute of Technology (MIT) and Harvard University in 1916, after only one year, the usual minimum time for the process being two years.

By this time the United States was at war with Germany, and Bush, like many other engineers, became involved with the development of military devices. Among other things, he worked on the construction of a submarine detector which utilised the effect of the ship's steel hull on a magnetic field.

After the Great War, Bush was seen as a very able research engineer and he was appointed as professor of electrical power transmission at the MIT. He soon became deeply involved with two kinds of problems. One was directly related to his work in power transmission, and it was concerned with being able to calculate precisely the distribution of electricity within a power network. This involved solving large systems of simultaneous linear equations, and was a difficult and time consuming mathematical task. One way to expedite this process would be to build a model of the network under consideration. To do this a machine, a computer, was needed which could produce an analogue of an electricity distribution system. To make such a machine was a lengthy process, but the MIT electrical engineering department produced such machines, and, indeed, machines of this type are now deemed absolutely necessary to control the flow of electricity in large networks.

Although work on this type of computer went on under Bush's influence, it was the second kind of problem which occupied his personal interest. The behaviour of electricity in thermionic valves, as used in radio receiving and transmission, was such that it could only be described in terms of rather intractable differential equations. The solution of these was impossible using direct methods and difficult using approximate numerical methods. The fact that so many difficulties arose because of these equations caused Bush to look for a practical means for their solution. Because he was essentially an electrical engineer it was not surprising that he should look for an electrical machine to accomplish his task.

Bush's first computer was called 'A Continuous Integraph' and it was built and fully operational before January 1927. It was constructed to evaluate integrals which contained a product and were of the form

$F(x) = \int_a^x f_1(x) . f_2(x) dx$, where $f_1(x) f_2(x)$ is a product of two functions of x.

To do this it used as its basic component an Elihu Thomson electricity meter of the kind found in all our homes. These normally work out how much electricity we have used so that the Electricity Board can send us a bill. In principle they measure the current and voltage and integrate their product, power (kilowatts) with respect to time (hours). The two electrical quantities (inputs) produce a rotation of a disc and pointers (output). The meter which Bush used was greatly altered and adapted to its purpose, and the machine which was built round it was quite large; it bore no resemblance to a thing which an amateur inventor might produce in his garden shed one Sunday afternoon. There were two input tables, one for each function, and one output table, which contained a linkage to multiply the integral by a further function of x if this was needed. Both the inputs and the output were graphs of functions of x which were transformed into or out of electrical currents and potential and mechanical measurement. Potentiometers were used to adjust the machine to suit the equation being solved, and a servo-electric motor was used to transform the disc output of the kilowatt hour meter into an effect which could be used to plot the output graph.

Bush obtained both accurate and useful results with the continuous integraph, but it was limited to the solution of first order differential equations. A new machine was planned almost immediately to solve second order equations. Later the same year, 1927, the first computer was modified for this purpose by adding a further integrating unit. However, this could not be another electricity meter because it proved impossible to turn the rotating disc output of the first meter into a means of accurately generating the current for the input of the second one. Instead, the Maxwell-Thomson device was invoked. The rotation for the meter was just what was required to rotate the disc of a mechanical integrator. Unfortunately, as soon as a load was placed on the moving parts of the machine its accuracy dropped. Since Bush was using the computer as a means of solving his very real engineering problems, accuracy was of paramount importance. Eventually he was able to solve the problem of connecting the two integrators together by using a servo-electric motor, as he had for the output system of his first device.

The new integraph worked well, being capable of all that the first version was and able to solve most second order differential equations with an overall error of between one and two per cent. Kelvin's suggested machine had been brought into reality by Bush. The engineer and the physicist now had an accurate means of solving many of their mathematical problems. The machine took a lot of preparation before a solution could be found and it did require several skilled operators. Also a considerable amount of mathematical manipulation and engineering design was required to bring the problem and a suitable machine configuration together. However, an analogue computer had been made which was both useful and highly accurate; this inspired Bush and his team to better things.

It is always easy to discover the overall limitations of a new machine. There were certain problems that this second machine would simply not be capable of tackling and these were known while it was being built. Differential equations of orders greater than two, those involving differential coefficients of $\dfrac{d^3y}{dx^3}$ (third order) and $\dfrac{d^4y}{dx^4}$ (fourth order) and so on could not be solved. Such equations were not as common in science as the second order ones, but they were usually extremely difficult to solve. Nor was this machine capable of handling systems of simultaneous differential equations of the second order, which arose more commonly. To tackle these a new machine was needed, one like Kelvin's dream, where integrator after integrator could be connected together: a true differential analyser.

To make such a computer was easier said than done, because although the servomotor had partially solved the problem that stopped Kelvin, it was troublesome when transmitting large magnifications of turning force (torque) which were required even in the modified integraph. It tended to be difficult to set properly and it even oscillated quite wildly at times. However, a new device came on the scene. This was a torque amplifier invented by C. W. Nieman of the Bethle-hem Steel Co. in 1927. It was used to magnify the input to an integrator. The torque amplifier worked on the principle of the marine capstan. The input shaft turns a drum on which a cord is wrapped; the angle with which the cord meets the drum determines the force which the drum transmits to it. This cord is connected to a stouter cord on an output drum, which is connected to the output shaft. The actual amplifying force comes from a motor which applies a constant, but op-posite torque to each of the two drums. In theory, the ampli-fication is given by $e^{\mu\theta}$, where e is the exponential number, μ is the coefficient of sliding friction and θ is the angle at which the cord meets the drum.

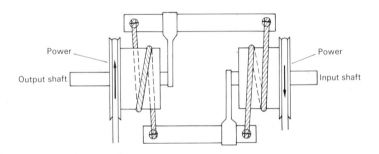

Nieman assisted Bush with the adaptation of his device during the building of a new computer. After some difficulties in preventing the amplifier from oscillating, it became relatively easy to obtain amplification factors in excess of 10,000, a necessary requirement for accurate results.

With torque amplifiers there was no limit to the number of integrators which could be connected together and Bush's new machine truly lived up to its name 'The Differential Analyser'. This, the first of a new and short-lived breed of computers, had six integrators. It could be used to solve most of the systems of ordinary differential equations which the engineers were likely to meet, including systems of two or three simul-taneous second order equations. The inputs and outputs were the same as the earlier machines, but the increase in scale and the addition of the torque amplifiers gave the computer a look of vast complexity. Indeed, it required a large room to house it. It was a complex mass of interconnected long metal axles, gears, discs, handles and electric motors.

Even to those who understood its principles and had designed and built it, it looked like something made with a gigantic Meccano set. This fact was noted in 1933 by a famous visiting British mathematician, D. R. **Hartree** of Manchester University, who, on his return to England, built a small-scale differential analyser using Meccano parts. This, the first of a number of small-scale professional models worked well with a high degree of accuracy. It was often used as a test bed for ideas which were later built into the full-size Manchester analyser. Hartree's Meccano analyser was an important triumph for British inventiveness and as well as its description in a scientific journal in 1935, it was the subject of a very proud article in the ill-fated and largely forgotten *Meccano Magazine* in June 1934.

Bush's analyser was an immediate success. Soon after its description was published late in 1931, universities in America and other countries began to experiment along similar lines. The fruits of this work were usually called differential analysers, after the name Bush had given to this form of computer. In particular, the Moore School of Electrical Engineering at the University of Pennsylvania ordered a copy of Bush's machine to fulfil very much the same purpose as the original machine: the solution of mathematical problems arising in engineering. A second copy was also requested by the Ordnance Department of the US Army for use at their Ballistics Research Laboratory at the Aberdeen Proving Ground, Maryland.

This second request was of particular significance. With the advent of modern warfare and the development of precision gunnery, mathematics has lurked in the background of all battles. It is necessary to know the precise trajectory of a shell, and the behaviour of a bomb after it leaves an aeroplane. Again, these problems frequently involve differential equations, the solution of which by numerical methods was an arduous and time-consuming task for ballistic experts. At least two first-rate mathematicians, J. E. Littlewood in England and Norbert Weiner in the United States, were occupied with this task during the Great War. Norbert Wiener was also at the MIT and was a colleague and close friend of

Bush for a long time. Wiener wrote a mathematical appendix to one of Bush's books on electrical circuit theory and he made a number of suggestions concerning the power distribution circuit analyser already mentioned. As we shall see, the differential analyser was by no means the end of the military part of the story.

Following his initial success with the Meccano differential analyser, Hartree was able to persude Sir Rupert McDougall, a wealthy businessman, to put up the money for a full-scale differential analyser to be built for the University of Manchester. Metropolitan Vickers Electrical Co. Ltd., with Bush as a consultant, built this analyser which had eight integrators and it was installed in the university in 1935. A machine of similar capacity was built at Cambridge University in 1939. A twelve integrator computer was constructed in Oslo, and one fairly similar to Bush's original design is believed to have been erected in Leningrad.

Although the differential analyser was an important and successful machine, it was by no means perfect. It took several days for the operators to set the connections between the rods and integrators and to adjust the gear ratios which represented the constants in the equations. This was acceptable when a set of problems was large enough to occupy the analyser for weeks, but for shorter problems it was an expensive and time-consuming task. The upshot of this was a new machine which overcame these difficulties and extended the power of the differential analyser approach beyond that of any other machine intended or even visualised.

However, about the time when this was happening, the career of Bush took several advances. In 1932 he was appointed vice president of MIT and dean of its engineering school. His administrative skills and expertise in handling people and committees at a very high level were recognised. A few years later he was appointed president of the Carnegie Institution in Washington. This was part of the foundation originally devoted to the administration of the vast fortune accumulated by Andrew Carnegie, the newspaper magnate and industrialist, to facilitate the furtherance of knowledge. In this new capacity Bush supervised the administration of all manner of schemes, large-scale experiments and the building and equipping of new laboratories. Indeed, in this position he became one of the most influential members of the American scientific establishment. So much was this the case, that by the outbreak of the Second World War he was scientific adviser to President Franklin D. Roosevelt. States of America. In this capacity, at a meeting on the 9th October 1941, he played a very important part in persuading the President to instigate the development of the atomic bomb. This, which became known as the Manhattan Project, was only part of the work of which Bush was in overall control as head of the national wartime scientific administration, the Office of Scientific Research and Development. Except for his design of a code breaking machine which was used with great effect against the Japanese codes, Bush was now an administrator and not a front-line research scientist like J. Robert Oppenheimer, the director of the research that culminated in the building of the first atomic bomb. However, his wartime association with the atomic projects, his very high position in the scientific community and his knowledge of the Washington administration made him a natural choice for membership of the various committees which were responsible for the development and control of atomic energy in post-war America. In these turbulent days of the 'Cold War', and the anti-communist witch hunts of Senator Joseph McCarthy when a kind of remorse was felt by the scientists responsible, and the country at large, for the development of the devastating weapon, Bush took on the chairmanship of the new Research and Development Board, with a considerable role in national defence. When criticism was commonplace, very little came his way, as befitted a man who was respected by all: scientists, administrators and politicians. Bush was a firm proponent of the uses of atomic energy and in some of his later books, particularly *Endless Horizons*, he envisaged a world which benefited immeasurably from the peaceful uses of a force that had first been unleashed in anger.

To return to the new machine; it was on an immense scale, weighing over one hundred tons, and it must truly have been the greatest of all the differential analysers built. The Maxwell-Thomson integrators and connecting axles remained, but almost everything else was altered. The important advance was that the problem-solving configuration was set automatically in three to five minutes. Most of the new ideas were electronic; the torque amplifiers had been replaced by very advanced servomechanisms called angle indicators and the constants were set by intricate, automatically-operated gear boxes. But most important of all was that the directors for the arrangement of the computer were fed into the machine by three punched paper tapes. Tape A gave instructions for the interconnecting of the integrators, tape B set the gear ratios and tape C gave the initial conditions necessary for the solution of the differential equations under specific conditions. The input was by a similar principle, but much improved version, to that used in the earlier machines. The output, however, was digital; it was a printout of numerical values which was a major advancement in accuracy and usefulness. The whole machine was built in three sections and independent problems could be processed simultaneously. It was originally intended that there would be thirty integrators, but Bush's description indicates that it was still working with eighteen integrators in 1945.

For a computer, in 1940, which could be set up in minutes and deal with complex problems (and many simultaneously) to an accuracy of one part in 10,000, there was only one field of operation. The new differential analyser spent the war years behind locked doors handling top secret work. During this period it was no doubt improved and adapted, and the 1945 published description includes these changes. That this machine represents the zenith of the differential analyser, and that it contributed enormously to the war effort is beyond doubt. It must also have shown its designers and operators the shortcomings of this type of computer while at the same time showing off the advantages of much of the controlling electronic equipment. If this new differential analyser had been equal to all problems, even with differential equations, it might have been the first of a new breed of computers, rather than the greatest of all the old ones.

The computers which have been described have all been attributed to Vannevar Bush, but it is obvious that he could not have been responsible for every aspect of every machine. Along with the relatively junior engineers, scientists, technicians and craftsmen who were involved in the detailed work, Bush collaborated with a number of senior colleagues, notably

S. H. Caldwell, who played a very large part in building the last machine, H. L. Hazen, F. D. Gage and H. R. Stewart.

Bush retired in 1955 and devoted all his time to those activities he had previously fitted around his academic and administrative duties. These included running a turkey farm, a deep interest in boats and boating and a passion for inventing. On the 1st July 1974, at the age of 84, he died from a stroke.

Meanwhile, in England, D. R. Hartree attempted to apply the differential analyser to even more complicated types of equations than had previously been attempted. These partial differential equations are of considerable importance in physics in the transmission of heat, electricity and especially shock waves. That he was not entirely successful gives us one clue as to why the days of the differential analyser were numbered. As we shall see in the next chapter, a new breed of computer was already being developed which could, with suitable planning, be used to solve all problems of this type. It would seem that the Americans, even with the new Bush anlyser, also experienced little success in solving partial differential equations, since the design of the atomic bomb involved the consideration of the mathematics of shock waves, and would require this. The computation of the solutions of these using skilled but tedious numerical techniques was undertaken for thousands of values. After the war, calculations of this kind were of great importance and the computers which were capable of doing them achieved precedence, but this is only part of the reason.

Differential analysers of the Bush type were in operation during the late 1940s and they finally reached their demise during the early 1950s. The engineer's differential equations did not go away however, and the concept of the differential analyser did not die. Also during the Second World War there were vast developments in electronics through research into radar and the control of aeroplanes and weapons. One outcome of this work was the electronic operational amplifier, which was developed by F. C. Williams in Britain. The coupling of a capacitor in parallel with this device made a successful integrator, which was a very definite substitute for the Maxwell-Thomson disc integrator. Operational amplifiers proved themselves capable of all the requirements for the solution of ordinary differential equations. Potentiometers again took on the role which they filled in Bush's continuous integraph. High-order ordinary differential equations and large systems of simultaneous differential equations could by modelled by electricity much more cheaply than by mechanical movements. The electrical analogue computer now fills the limited role of the differential analyser in engineering. Even large analogue computers, with a great number of operational amplifiers which can act as integrators, exist in some engineering laboratories, notably those connected with the aircraft industry.

ENIAC. (Photo: *The Smithsonian Institution.*)

CHAPTER EIGHT

John W. Mauchly and J. Presper Eckert

WHILE BUSH and his colleagues were busy building their analogue machines, a number of other groups of computer builders became active. However, they took a different line of approach in their enterprises. The differential analysers in effect were a model of the problem, and somewhere in the process of finding the numerical solution measurements were performed, as in the number of turns of a shaft, a distance on a graph, or the magnitude of a voltage. The alternative to a measuring machine is a counting device, and this was the approach that developed during the 1930s.

In 1937, Howard H. **Aiken** began to consider the building of a large-scale computer. Aiken was a graduate research student and an instructor in the Department of Physics at Harvard University. Like Bush, he became involved with a large set of differential equations which could not be solved by direct mathematical methods and whose solution by approximate numerical techniques involved a monumental amount of labour. Unlike Bush, he looked towards extending the punched card counting machines of IBM, which had developed from Hollerith's enterprising work. Aiken set out to convince his superiors of the worth of such a machine and to find the facilities and the wherewithal to construct it. In the course of this he wrote a report which outlined his ideas, and in particular gave four points of difference between punched-card accounting machines and calculating devices which would be useful in scientific work. These points are: that whereas accounting machines handle only positive numbers, scientific machines must be able to handle negative ones as well; that scientific machines must be able to handle such functions as logarithms, sines, cosines and a whole lot of other functions; the computer would be most useful for scientists if, once it was set in motion, it would work through the problem frequently for numerous numerical values without intervention until the calculation was finished. and that the machine should compute lines instead of columns, which is more in keeping with the sequence of mathematical events.

Aiken's report came to the attention of Professor T. H. Brown at Harvard, who had connections with IBM. Eventually it was arranged that Aiken would work at IBM with a group of senior engineers (C. D. Lake, F. E. Hamilton and B. M. Durfee) on a new machine based on his ideas. Aiken's machine, the Automatic Sequence Controlled Calculator (ASCC) was principally mechanical, but driven by electricity; many of its major components were electromechanical counters. There were many magnetically operated switches. The input was from punched cards and the output was also by this means or by a typewriter. The sequence mechanism which governed the order in which tasks were carried out was controlled by punched tape. The tape carried three types of instructions: where the data being used was stored; where the result was to be stored; and the operation which was to be performed on the data. It is not entirely coincidental that these kinds of instructions were somewhat similar to those envisaged by Babbage as being needed for the analytical engine. Aiken was greatly influenced by this early pioneer and frequently read many of Babbage's works. He considered the ASCC to be the complete realisation of Babbage's plans for the analytical engine.

The finished machine was 51 feet long and 8 feet high. It operated on 23 significant figures and it had 60 constant registers, 72 adding storage registers and a central multiplying and dividing unit. It performed an addition in six seconds and a division in twelve seconds. There were electromechanical tables for logarithms (and antilogarithms) in base 10 and for sines. The ASCC was built at the IBM development laboratories at Endicott. It was first used in January 1943 but it was then moved to Harvard University, where it came into use in May 1944. The following August, Thomas J. Watson, President of IBM gave the ASCC to Harvard, where it became known as the Harvard Mark 1 and was quickly pressed into service for the US Navy.

The connection between Aiken and IBM then broke up, and each severed branch contributed a new stream of machines. From Aiken there were Harvard Marks 2, 3 and 4 up to 1952, the later designs using thermionic valves even though Aiken clung to electromechanical methods longer than many of his colleagues and contemporaries. We shall see why this was so later. IBM also built a further number of electromechanical machines, culminating in the Selective Sequence Electronic Calculator (SSEC). This massive machine was very much in the Aiken tradition, but it used electronic valves in its arithmetic unit. It was one of the great giants of the period of the individual machines. Work on it began in 1945 and it was also built at Endicott. On its completion it was moved to the IBM building in New York, where it was dedicated in January 1948. The SSEC was the first computer to do many things which are now commonplace, but it soon became obvious that it was the end of an old line, rather than the beginning of a new one, and it was dismantled in 1952 after only five years of use.

As well as IBM, Bell Telephone Laboratories began work on counting, or digital computers. It was natural that the research equipment of a telephone company should use the commonplace components which it made and used. George **Stibnitz** a senior engineer at the Laboratories, began experimenting with electromagnetic relays at home in his spare time after he became aware of the possibilities they offered while he was designing the magnetic elements for them. Relays and switching mechanisms which are operated automatically by electrical pulses are found in their thousands in automatic telephone exchanges where they connect the caller with the number he requires, using the pulses emitted from his own telephone handset in the course of dialling. Stibnitz soon soldered together banks of relays which would perform addition. A relay computer was obviously a practical possibility. There was also no shortage of problems for it to solve, particularly from two groups within the laboratory, one on the theory of electrical filters and the other on power transmission lines. From each of the two groups came large quantities of calculations involving complex numbers. These are numbers made up from two parts, such as 3 and 5 and the square root of -1 i.e. $\sqrt{-1}$, commonly known as i, in the form $3 + 5i$. The multiplication and division of one of these numbers by another involves several times the work of ordinary multiplication and division, so these seemed suitable tasks for the computer to perform. The Complex Number Computer was begun in late 1937 or early 1938 and it was in service in 1938. Further relay computers, of increasing complexity, were built by Bell Telephone Laboratories, including two machines for the Ballistic Research Laboratory at the Aberdeen Proving Ground.

It is importnt to note that the Aiken and IBM machines also relied fairly heavily on electromagnetic relays of the kind used by Stibnitz.

By the 1930s, electronics was a comparatively well-developed branch of engineering, with quite advanced radio transmitters and receivers in operation and equipment using similar techniques found in scientific laboratories. In effect, the thermionic valve was a well-known device having many forms and many purposes. Why then had computers so far used mechanical or electromechanical elements? Perhaps the simplest answer is that the properties of mechanical systems were predictable and that large systems such as heavy engines or complex telephone exchanges had proved themselves reliable. Bush knew the properties of large systems of steel and Stibnitz knew the reliability of the telephone network. Electronic valves, however, were subject to stresses during the warming up period, and the changes in temperature eventually caused wires to break. The lifetime of a valve was, at best, known only statistically; there was no real means of knowing whether a particular valve would fail or not at any time, and so there was no means of knowing whether a piece of electronic equipment would function when it was switched on. In practice, electronic systems contained a fairly small number of valves and so failures could be detected and quickly repaired. Statistically, the failure rate of a piece of electronic equipment is likely to be related to the number of active components it possesses. A piece of equipment with 1,000 valves was more likely to break down than one with only 10 valves. Detection of the fault was also a greater problem in the larger system. The advantage that valves had over relays was that they operated instantly. However, the engineers and scientists were only just getting used to the idea of doing a problem in seconds which had previously taken hours with a human calculator. There was, as yet, no need for increased speed. It was left to those who were interested in both computing and electronics to make the first move in the new directions; this could certainly have been made at least a decade earlier if there had been a need or incentive. Indeed, it is believed that J. W. Bryce of IBM had carried out work on electronic mechanisms for accounting machines. Actual electronic counters had been devised in 1919 by E. H. Eccles and F. W. Jordan and a binary counter had been developed at Cambridge by C. E. Wynn-Williams in 1932. Devices for counting radio activity and cosmic radiation were also made by scientists during the 1930s.

The first person credited with making an electronic computer was John V. **Atanasoff**. He was an associate professor of mathematics and physics at Iowa State College (now University) from 1926. His work, like that of many others we have heard about, was concerned with differential equations. This caused him to investigate the computing methods already in use. He thought differential analysers of the Bush type were clumsy and difficult to use and rather limited in their applications, so he sought to find an easier way to automatic computation. Atanasoff spent some time, after abandoning his analogue approach, investigating the possibilities of various types of electric circuitry. During 1937 and 1938 he developed a design for a digital electronic computer which possessed logic circuits and a memory. With the help of C. E. **Berry** and a grant from the State of Iowa, he put together a prototype device which was operating by the end of 1939, which showed the possibilities of the electronic approach to computing.

The Atanasoff-Berry computer was to be a machine with a special purpose. It was to solve simultaneous linear equations. Pairs of equations, such as

$$2x + 3y = 1$$
$$x - 2y = 4$$

are frequently found in school examinations and are easily solved. These were not quite what Atanasoff had in mind; he envisaged systems of thirty equations each with thirty un-knowns. It was possible and necessary to solve these equations by ordinary mathematics, but it was very tedious and time-consuming.

Only certain circuits were to contain valves; the memory, which could have used them, was made up from rotating drums each containing rows of paper capacitors. A charged capacitor held one element of information. Several elements of information would make up one number or sign for the computer. Since the charge on a capacitor leaks away by itself, it was necessary that the contents of the memory were re-newed periodically. That Atanasoff did not completely trust the reliability of valves was one reason for their somewhat restricted use; nevertheless, his machine was to contain over 300 of them; one of the largest systems of valves that had yet been used. The binary code was to be the means of repre-senting quantities which were to be put into the machine with the aid of punched cards. They also formed a memory for intermediate results. In fact, this piece of machinery did not work well and the computer was basically unrealiable, although the electronic part was successful. Serious compu-tation was never possible, and it was soon realised that the machine was limited in concept, design and usefulness. It was, perhaps, one of the failures for computing, yet one of the great successes for electronics. In 1942, both Atanasoff and Berry left Iowa State College, the former for the Naval Ord-nance Laboratory where he went on to do valuable war work connected with electronic systems. The Atanasoff-Berry ma-chine was thus abandoned; no one else was prepared to com-plete it and make it both fully operational and reliable.

During the active period of construction of this machine, Atanasoff was visited by a physicist who already had an in-terest in the counting circuits. This visitor was one of the principals of our story, John W. Mauchly. John **Mauchly** was born in Cincinnati, Ohio on the 30th August 1907. He at-tended schools in Washington DC and in 1925 he obtained a scholarship from the State of Maryland to attend Johns Hop-kins University to read engineering. After two years, his in-terests changed in the direction of pure science and he gained a degree in physics. In 1932 he gained a doctorate in physics and obtained an academic position to teach this subject. He taught physics in a number of colleges. Also he spent time carrying out research at the laboratory of the Department of Terrestrial Magnetism at the Carnegie Institution, which embraced a wider sphere of research than its title suggests. During the beginning of the Second World War, Mauchly was a physics teacher on the staff of Ursinus College, a fairly small institution on the outskirts of Philadelphia. It was from this time that his interest in electronic calculators developed. Although a physicist, he retained a strong interest in electronic engineering and he took an interest in the development of new circuits. He made visits, often with his senior students, to laboratories where counting circuits were being developed and used. One such visit was to the Bartol Research Foundation where electronic equipment was counting cosmic rays. Also while at Ursinus College, he built a number of experimental counting circuits to test his ideas. Certainly, Mauchly had some very firm ideas for an electronic computer before he visited Atanasoff. When the visit took place at Ames, Iowa, the two pioneers had an involved discussion, with Mauchly's concept of an electronic computer being somewhat different to that of the Atanasoff-Berry machine, since he believed that greater speeds were attainable than this machine was capable of realising. A great amount was also learned by Mauchly about Atanasoff's ideas for digital computers and about his experience gained in building his special purpose machine.

In the summer of 1941 Mauchly went to the Moore School of Electrical Engineering at the University of Pennsylvania, to take a defence training course in electronics. Shortly after finishing the course he was offered a post as an assistant professor at the Moore School. When he joined the faculty he hoped for sympathy for his ideas, but he found that most of those who were likely to show an interest were fully occupied either with urgent war work concerned with research, the training of people in electronics, or the use of the Bush analyser for ballistic calculations. Experience at the School had shown the Bush analyser to be an awkward tool. When large or related problems that could be set on the machine for weeks were to be solved it was in constant use, but when small problems were being dealt with, engineers found it more expedient to solve them mathematically, without taking days to set up the machine. However, with the work on ballistics in progress, the analyser was in constant use.

There was, however, one person who was not only prepared to listen to Mauchly's ideas, but was himself very interested in the whole idea of building an electronic computer. This was J. Presper **Eckert**. Eckert was born in 1919 in Philadelphia. He went to the William Penn Carter School at Germanstown. From there he entered the Moore School at the University of Pennsylvania as an undergraduate in 1937. It was shortly after his graduation in 1941 that he and Mauchly became acquainted. Eckert was a very talented student and he was pressed into service as an instructor almost immediately after he graduated. He was one of the laboratory instructors on the defence course that Mauchly took in 1941. During the course, Mauchly took the opportunity to talk to him about his ideas on electronic computing nearly every day. The two became great friends and colleagues, but the military work which went on alongside teaching duties was pressing. Eckert was eventually involved with work on ultraviolet light and the development of means of measuring metal fatigue. Later, he went on to develop a method for measuring small magnetic fields to be used in detecting marine mines. He then went on to work on the electronics of radar and target locating and following equipment; these devices played a decisive part in weaponry, and their development and construction was considered to be of the very highest priority.

In August 1941 Mauchly set down in a fairly short document his thoughts on the idea for an electronic computer, in which he envisaged such a machine as having considerable advantages over the Bush Analyser, particularly with regard to speed and ease of use. Even though the analyser was continually in service it was no match for the requirements of the military.

By this time a group of people at the Moore School formed part of the Ballistic Research Laboratory. This consisted of a number of people from Aberdeen and some members of the School's staff. They were operating the analyser and training people to carry out ballistic calculations; not all at a high level, some were being prepared for tedious years of routine arithmetical computation. In order to organise the somewhat diverse and uncoordinated activities, the Ordnance Department of the US Army who ran the Ballistic Research Laboratory at the Aberdeen Proving Grounds, Maryland, assigned Lt. Herman H. Goldstine to take charge of all the ballistics activities. Before the war Goldstine had been an assistant professor of mathematics at the University of Michigan. When he was called to service in July 1942 his expertise was soon appreciated, and the following month he was sent to Aberdeen; at the end of September 1942 he was sent to look after the Philadelphia set up.

Goldstine read Mauchly's report and was quickly seduced by Mauchly's promise of much higher speeds in computing for an electronic device. He approached the Director of Moore School, J. G. Brainerd, in March 1943 and found that he agreed with Mauchly's ideas and was willing for the School to become involved with the construction of an electronic computer. Goldstine then took the idea for the project to his superiors, together with a formal proposal from Brainerd. After passing through military channels and the plethora of committees whose approval was necessary to begin such an enterprise, it finally came to the notice of Oswald Veblen on the 9th April 1943. He was a professor at Princeton and one of the greatest American mathematicians. Veblen is reputed to have said to the Director of the Ballistics Research Laboratory, Col. L. E. Simon, 'Simon, give Goldstine the money'. Thereafter, events moved quickly, with the Ordnance Department giving almost immediate approval. Work on the ENIAC (Electronic Numerical Integrator and Computer) began on the 31st May 1943.

Eckert, who was just about to gain his masters degree in electrical engineering, was appointed chief engineer of the project and responsible for the design of the electronic circuits. Mauchly was the consultant to the enterprise, and saw that his ideas were realised in hardware. Brainerd was the nominal director and handled much of the administration and the necessary dealings with the authorities. Goldstine was appointed as the representative of the Ballistics Research Laboratory and was quite deeply involved with all the work, but his main role was that of liaison officer, matching the accomplishments of the Moore School with the demands of the Ballistics Research Laboratory. ENIAC was to be designed as a general purpose machine, but its primary purpose was to be the compilation of firing tables from the computation of bomb and shell trajectories.

The construction of ENIAC did not simply begin at the beginning and continue until it was finished. First, although Mauchly, Eckert and the others involved were highly optimistic of the outcome, there was no guarantee that their ideas would transfer directly into electronic hardware. Also the needs of the Ballistic Research Laboratory tended to change with the progress of the war. The first real milestone reached was the construction of two electronic accumulators which were to carry out part of the arithmetic processing. When these proved capable of solving certain equations, technically known as second order difference equations, the inventors knew they were on the right track.

How had they solved the problem of the reliability of the thermionic valves? It was the cunning of Presper Eckert which made the breakthrough. Electronic components: valves, resistors, capacitors etc., have tolerances of operation for which they are specifically designed. Quantities such as voltage and current have to fall within a certain range for the components to work efficiently without burning out. Eckert simply reduced these quantities; for valves, no voltage had to exceed half of the stated maximum and no current had to exceed a quarter of this. He hoped to gain a lifetime of 2,500 hours for each valve.

Initially, the ENIAC was to contain about 5,000 valves and have one crude memory made up from switches and ten accumulators. This was to cost $150,000. When it was completed, due to the demands of the Ballistic Research Laboratory, it contained 18,000 valves and had three function memories and twenty accumulators at a total cost of $400,000.

The construction of ENIAC owed quite a lot to the logical arrangement of the Bush Differential Analyser. Initially ENIAC was intended to accomplish the same task but at a much faster speed. Indeed, this was precisely the point which was presented to the Ballistics Research Laboratory and the Army Ordnance authorities to convince them of its value. The method of counting, however, was similar to that used in Aiken's Harvard Mark 1 and other machines of that type. What he and others had accomplished with electromagnetic wheel counters, where an electric current magnetised a piece of iron which in turn operated a mechanical device and advanced a circular counter as many times as it experienced an electric pulse, Eckert accomplished with electronic valves. A direct electronic analogue of these counters was produced; these were the 'ring counters'. Eckert's electronic calculators worked in base ten, not in binary arithmetic as might reasonably be assumed from subsequent developments. This was partly because somewhere along the line binary numbers would have to be converted into denary numbers, and also because of the parallel design of the ENIAC, where several aspects of the computation could take place at once and not necessarily in direct sequence, and it was assessed that more valves and other components would be needed to make a binary machine.

Instructions were set using masses of switches on function tables (which also served as a slow memory) and by numerous interconnections of one component with another using plug-in wires. In all, the ENIAC had the appearance of a vast jungle of wires. Those quantities and commands which were required at a particular time were stored in the machine in a very small and expensive memory composed of valves. Several valves were required to store each digit. The input and output used punched cards, and cards also served as a long-term memory to store intermediate results. The contents of cards had to be used over and over again for each sequence of calculations. By todays standards these were read in at a very slow rate, 100 cards per minute. The input and output units were not constructed at the Moore School, but were built by IBM. IBM were not told what kind of machine they were building parts for; they were only given the specifications, but no doubt their engineers must have been very curious.

The electronic processes were kept in synchronisation by sending a heartbeat of 100,000 pulses of electricity per second through its operating circuits. The whole coordination of the machine in solving the problem was maintained by means of a device called the 'master programmer'. As a piece of electronic hardware ENIAC contained about 18,000 valves, 6,000 switches, 70,000 resistors and 10,000 capacitors. All this consumed a very hefty 140 kilowatts of power. The computer was about 100 feet long, 3 feet wide and 10 feet high and was in the form of a U-shape made up of 40 panels. The numbers it handled had ten digits.

Even with Eckert's philosophy of electronic design, the ENIAC could not be expected to run faultlessly from being switched on. Valves would blow and a myriad of other types of problems would always be likely to develop. What was important was to have runs of several hours or days without a breakdown, when problems which would have taken months or years otherwise could be solved. Likewise, it was thought good if the ratio of operating time was high compared with the time required for maintenance or repairs. At the Moore School they were eventually able to expect the ENIAC to work accurately for 90 per cent of the time, a staggering achievement considering its complexity. It was later reported from the Ballistics Research Laboratory at Aberdeen, that they experienced much worse results, only achieving operation for 50 per cent of the time. This was eventually found to be because they switched the ENIAC off each day when they had finished computing. In fact, it was very important to keep it switched on for the whole time, 24 hours a day, because the heating and cooling of valve filaments was one of the main causes of deterioration, resulting in valve failures and consequent breakdowns. Apparently at Aberdeen the operators had been ordered to switch it off to reduce the electricity bills, and because any machinery switched on and not in use had to be guarded.

After two and a half years of work, in which a number of designers, technicians and craftsmen had participated as well as the principals, the ENIAC was ready. Unfortunately, this was about three months after the end of the war which it had been designed to help win. This was, however, of little consequence. It was to be a computational workhorse for the nation and as such it was classified highly secret; already people wished to use it to solve involved and very hush-hush problems.

During its construction another important person came into the story. John **von Neumann**, who was without doubt one of the greatest of all twentieth century mathematicians, and about whom we will read much more later, was employed as a consultant to both the Ballistics Research Laboratory at Aberdeen and the Manhattan Project at Los Alamos, New

Mexico, where the development of the world's first nuclear weapons was being carried out. Johnny, as he was known to his friends, arranged for a group of important problems from Los Alamos to be solved by the ENIAC at the Moore School after its completion. That these problems were important after the end of the war suggests that they were not related to the first atomic weapons. However, since Edward Teller, one of the scientists who advocated and developed the hydrogen thermonuclear bomb, was involved in the background, it is reasonable to suggest that this very secret and highly important first task for the ENIAC was concerned with this weapon.

As an aside, much of the computation involved in the solution of the partial differential equations for the first atom bombs was carried out at the Los Alamos site with a whole bank of IBM punched-card calculators. Richard Feynman, who was later to become a Nobel Laureate in physics, was in charge of this enterprise for part of the time. He speeded up the calculation process by arranging the IBM machines in sequence so that one machine dealt with one aspect of the calculation, another with another aspect and so on. In this way he was able to compute solutions in only a fraction of the time that had otherwise been required, and to process several problems at the same time.

The first set of calculations for ENIAC began in November or December 1945 and the Los Alamos problem, which served as a very full test for the machine, using over 95 per cent of its circuitry, was concluded during the early months of 1946. It was found it could do one addition or subtraction in 200 μs ($\frac{1}{5,000}$ of a second), a multiplication in 3μs ($\frac{3}{1,000}$ sec. or 0·003 sec) and a division or the extraction of a square root, for which there was a combined piece of the computer, in 30 μs (0·03 sec.). The operation of multiplication was not performed by the now familiar method of repeated addition; it was carried out with the help of a built-in multiplication table. It was certainly obvious by the time the first calculations were performed, if not long before the computer was finished, that the setting up of problems for solution was complicated, tedious and time-consuming. Whole banks of switches had to be set, lengths of cable had to be interconnected to various panels or components, often as much as 80 feet apart, and the very limited internal memories had to be taken into account in preparing a suitable sequence of actions for reducing the number of times intermediate results had to be re-entered into the machine.

The ENIAC stayed at the Moore School longer than was intended. It occupied quite a large amount of space, and a new building was being prepared at Aberdeen to take it and the auxiliary computing facilities. This building was not ready by the 30th June 1946, when ENIAC was formally accepted by the US Army. Von Neumann and other government scientific advisers expressed a desire to have America's only computer in operation at that time since it was occupied with work of national importance; in other words, they did not want it out of action for many months when there was still a pressing military need for it. Remember, this was the beginning of a period of mutual distrust between America and Britain and the countries of Eastern Europe. Finally, on the 9th November 1946 ENIAC was switched off and the process of transferring it to the BRL at Aberdeen began. It was switched on again on the 29th July 1947 and it continued in operation at Aberdeen until 11.45pm on the 2nd October 1955. Calculations relating to ballistics and nuclear weapons were carried out on it (at least until Los Alamos got its own computer), and also research mathematicians from the universities were allowed access to its facilities. Parts of ENIAC, the world's first general purpose electronic computer, have since then been on show at the Smithsonian Institution in Washington, DC.

Ways of improving the design of an electronic computer were often learned before much of the hardware of ENIAC had been assembled. Shortcomings of the whole concept of the ENIAC were easy to spot in light of even the limited experience of the Moore group. However, it is rarely possible to make conceptual improvements once a machine is being constructed. Failures of the design were frequently modified in construction, or after testing or operation, but Mauchly and Eckert were stuck with the idea. It is not, therefore, surprising that their experience should suggest many ways in which they could make a new computer very different from ENIAC, and that they should want to build such a machine.

One way in which future computers should differ from their

first machine was that as many as possible of the instructions which a computer uses in the execution of its task should be stored within it, thus eliminating the need for all the switches, plugs and exterior cables which were such a characteristic part of the ENIAC.

The new computer planned was the EDVAC, Electronic Discrete Variable Computer. Much of the discussion of this machine we will leave to the chapter on von Neumann, since he, along with Mauchly and Eckert, was one of the originators of the new concept of an electronic computer which it embodied. However one important aspect of the design which is important to the narrative on Mauchly and Eckert was its memory.

Eckert, in particularly, began considering means of developing a memory in which the entirety of a computer's program could be stored. Atanasoff had worked with paper capacitors but these were certainly unsuitable for the machine to follow ENIAC. At first Eckert thought of a metal drum whose surface was divided into many cells, each of which contained a medium which could be magnetised in much the same way as ordinary recording tape. He soon realised that the rotation of the drum, which was needed to give access to the various cells, would cause the same disadvantages of speed, wear and friction that had limited the mechanical computers. During his days working on the developments of radar, Eckert had invented a very novel delay device. This came to his mind as just what was needed for an internal computer memory.

The new memory elements were, in effect, tanks about 1½ metres long containing mercury. At one end of the tank was a suitable quartz crystal. When an electric current impinged on this crystal it would alter its size and shape very slightly and only temporarily. This is known as the piezoelectric effect, so named from the Greek word piezin, to press. This temporary alteration in the crystal set up a disturbance in the memory, which travelled along the tank as a shock wave. At the other end of the tank there was a similar crystal which, when struck by the shock wave, emitted an electrical pulse. The important effect of the delay line was that it took a finite time for the wave to travel the length of the tank, not an instantaneous one (as when a current is conducted along a wire). By amplifying the electrical impulse emitted, it could be re-introduced to the delay line. Thus an electrical impulse could be preserved indefinitely as a shockwave, and hence, the electrical currents representing a computer program could be stored.

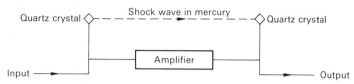

It was intended that the EDVAC would have a large bank of these mercury delay lines for its internal memory. As events turned out, Eckert and Mauchly left the Moore School long before this project was completed. Even von Neumann lost interest when he became involved in the building of another computer. In fact, the first operational stored program computer was the EDSAC, Electronic Delay Storage Automatic Computer, which was built along the lines of the EDVAC, but in England, at Cambridge by M. V. Wilkes.

Mauchly and Eckert left the University of Pennsylvania in October 1946 to start the Electronic Control Company. They received an order to build a computer BINAC, Binary Automatic Computer, for the Northrop Aircraft Company. It was somewhat similar to the design of the intended EDVAC but it came into use a lot sooner, in August 1950. A newly re-modelled company, the Eckert-Mauchly Computer Corporation went on to obtain the contract to build the UNIVAC, Universal Automatic Computer, for the National Bureau of Standards.

The economics, as well as the electronics, of computer building was also in its infancy and it proved very difficult to estimate the cost of computers and the time and resources needed to finish them. In the event, this new corporation fell into financial difficulties. At about the time that UNIVAC 1 came into operation in 1951, the corporation was taken over by Remington Rand. The two men then formed and operated the new UNIVAC Division of Remington Rand (later to become Sperry Rand). Further UNIVACs became the first commercially available electronic computers.

Mauchly and Eckert received many awards, medals and

honorary degrees throughout the 1960s. They continued to hold senior appointments in the UNIVAC Division at Sperry Rand for the rest of their working lives. John W. Mauchly died on January 8, 1980.

Konrad Zuse. (Photo: *With the kind permission of Prof. Dr. Konrad Zuse and by the courtesy of the Deutches Museum, Munich.*)

CHAPTER NINE

Konrad Zuse

WHILE THE large-scale computer developments were taking place in the USA and a little later in England, there was one person accomplishing considerable engineering feats in Germany. Konrad **Zuse**, working on his own, except for a few friends, created several computing machines and was responsible for a whole host of ideas before the start of the Second World War. Because of the political situation, these developments did not become known to the other pioneers, and it was only in the late 1940s that Zuse's important and sometimes pre-emptive work was known to have been carried out.

Konrad Zuse was born in 1910 in Berlin. He grew up in Braunsberg, East Prussia where he attended the Humanistisches Gymnasium. Following school, he went to the Technische Hochschule at Berlin-Charlottenburg to study civil engineering. It was in 1934, during his engineering studies, that he first became interested in calculating machines. Like so many other pioneers, he came up against a whole lot of important and necessary mathematical computations. When he wanted to be sampling the delights of Berlin, Konrad was having to spend his time working through the long statics calculations which are so important in the training of civil engineers, since they are involved in all buildings, bridges and tunnels. In fact, he was to go on to become an aeronautical engineer, where similar calculations occur in designing the wings and fuselage of an aeroplane.

Initially, Zuse's computing ideas were designed to save himself time, but soon he became actively involved in their development and he must have found he had less time than before. His first notion was concerned with attempting to design a form which could be used in conjunction with a punch. This gave very little improvement in the method of calculation but it helped to develop his idea of what is now a program, so he set to work to mechanise the process. Zuse had had a fascination for mechanical and practical things since his childhood; he harboured a childhood ambition to become an inventor. During the following years he formed a plan for his first computing machine the Z1, which was begun in 1936. This was mechanical in its operation. Its arithmetic unit consisted of a large number of two-state mechanical switches. A fairly large memory was made; this again was mechanical, working by means of the positions of a metal bar. The memory was built up in layers, with glass plates between each one. The whole unit was very compact, a cubic metre of such a memory was equivalent to a roomfull of electromechanical telephone relays. The program was carried on punched tape. The Z1 arithmetic unit did not work very well; the transmission of commands through mechanical linkages effectively proved impossible. However, the mechanical memory did live up to its expectation and a patent was applied for and granted in 1936.

The construction of the Z1 was carried out by Zuse in his spare time, He did receive some financial help from a calculating machine manufacturer, Dr Kurt Panke, but it was soon obvious that the two of them operated at different levels: Panke expected a machine on the well-established principles of mechanical calculators, whereas Zuse had an entirely new concept.

As it will be remembered, Babbage attempted to build his analytical machine mechanically and he ran into all kinds of trouble. How did Zuse succeed in principle at the first attempt? Apart from the obvious improvements in materials and techniques, the answer is simple: Zuse used the binary system. All his switches and memory devices had only to be two-state ones, such as could work by distinguishing a turn of a shaft from no turn, or left from right. In fairness to Babbage, Zuse aspired to use many less digits in his calculations.

Zuse's way forward was obvious: the mechanical arithmetic unit had to be abandoned. For the Z2 he replaced this with one built from electromechanical relays. He preserved the store from his first machine and incorporated it into the new computer. Another German pioneer worked on the Z2, Helmut Schreyer. Schreyer was very much an advocate of electrification and it was to this aspect of the Z2 that he was drawn. Also Schreyer worked on his own electronic ideas for computing and the two of them made an application to build a 2,000 valve device for the German government. This was turned down but an electric arithmetic unit was started. This, however, was also terminated due to wartime difficulties in 1942. It is perhaps important to realise that Schreyer's approach to electronic computers used logical processors rather than arithmetical ones as were used in the ENIAC.

In 1939 Zuse was called into military service. Schreyer and Panke attempted to get him released from the army. At first they did not succeed, but six months later when it was realised that he was an aeroplane engineer by profession, he was sent back to work at the Henschel Aircraft Works where he had earlier given up his job to work on his computers full-time. However, he could still work on his machines at weekends. He was thus able to finish the Z2. It was capable of efficiently working out simple formulae as presented through a program on punched tape. It was still very much an experimental machine and trouble was experienced with the rather substandard relays, but it had justified Zuse's ideas; now it was appropriate to build a machine to fulfil a useful purpose.

The Z2 impressed the authorities at the factory. Through them it came to the notice of the German Aeronautical Research Institite (DVL), Berlin-Adlershof. Although the poor quality of the relays meant that the demonstration was less than faultless, the ingenuity of the Z2 convinced the DVL that they should support Zuse and his next machine. This, the Z3, was to be a full-scale computer, not an experimental demonstration model. With the resources offered, the Z3 was constructed in the two years from 1939–41 at Berlin, Methfesselstrasse.

The full-scale machine had a very impressive relay arithmetic unit. The program was entered on punched tape. The input was by means of a keyboard, using four decimal places and a point and, the output was a lamp display. For once Zuse abandoned the mechanical memory and used relays instead. Altogether the Z3 contained 2,600 relays. It went straight into service for the German aircraft industry where it was used for solving sets of simultaneous equations with three unknowns, quadratic equations and mathematical entities associated with linear equations and complex numbers which were involved in calculations concerned with the vibration of airframes under stress. Unfortunately the Z3, like the Z1 and Z2, was destroyed in an air raid. However, it showed the way to an even better computer. A reconstruction of the Z3 was made in 1960, it can be seen at the Deutsches Museum in Munich.

By 1945, the Z4 was complete, in the sense that any computer was finished; later it was altered and modified. It was capable of processing simple programs and in many ways it was a refinement and expansion of the Z3, without many new concepts being incorporated. It is very interesting to note that its memory was again mechanical, no doubt the reliability and space saving of this type of mechanism was important. After being built in Berlin, the Z4 became an important possession of the Aerodynamic Research Institute at Gottingen, and as such was to be protected as the Russian Army approached the town in April 1945. The route that the lorry which carried it to safety followed was a long one. In order to avoid invading troops, it went round much of Germany until it was deemed safe to lay the precious computer in temporary retirement in the cellar of a house in Hinterstein in the Bavarian Alps, near the Austrian border. The Z4 was coded Versuchsmodell 4, or V4. Because of the Association of V4 with the V1 and V2 flying bombs and rockets, the British and American troops who eventually found it (it had not been found by the French who had entered the village first) were most surprised when their multifarious precautions were unnecessary and the fearsome V4 was just a conglomeration of mechanical bits and pieces.

After the war the Z4 was considerably improved and it was leased from Zuse for service with the Federal Technical University, Eidgenössische Technische Hochschule in Zurich. The mechanical memory worked so well that it was common practice to leave the Z4 operating unattended through the night; a very different state of affairs from that of the ENIAC. The machine stayed in Zurich from 1950 to 1955, when it was moved to The Research Laboratory, St. Louis near Basel.

This was a French aerodynamic research institution and the Z4 was again working the type of problems it was intended to solve. It continued in operation until 1960, a considerable time for a mechanical computer and five years longer than ENIAC.

The Z series of computers were not the only ones built by Zuse during the Second World War. As we have seen, his early career was intimately involved with the aircraft industry. During the hostilities, the Henschel Aircraft Works was producing remote-controlled aircraft. For one of these to fly the correct course, it had to be accurately produced with many measurements having to be set to within fine tolerances, Deviations from the design specifications had to be compensated for by the adjustment of the control surfaces. To achieve all of this, many actual measurements were performed on each craft and the compensations calculated. In fact, two banks of mechanical computers were operated night and day to achieve this. Zuse first devised a special purpose computer, the S1, to make the required computations when the dimensions of the aeroplane were fed into it. An improvement was made with the S2, where the measuring apparatus was actually a part of the computer, and the setting calculations were computed directly.

Zuse also built a machine to perform purely logical calculations, the L1. It was not at first obvious what purposes computers would fill and there were many experiments throughout Europe and the USA which used computers for purposes other than mathematical and business calculations. The L1 stemmed from Zuse's interest in logic and the very close connection between logical calculus and computer operation. Zuse was one of the first people to realise this connection. The L1 was intended as an experimental machine and this line of investigation was not pursued with further hardware.

Although Zuse was concerned about programming and the fundamentals of computer language since his earliest days of experimentation it was during the period of enforced rest from mechanical work after the end of the war that he put together many of the ideas which he had developed. His Plankalkül was one of the first computer languages. It was a very logical kind of language, being suitable for what we would now call 'artificial intelligence' as well as a mathematical calculation. Indeed, it was, perhaps, too orientated towards logical operations for it to survive. Like so many things which are first in the field, it was quickly bypassed by its successors which had extracted the useful parts of the original idea and jettisoned those which were not important. In this case, the highly successful successor was ALGOL, ALGOrhythmic Language.

After the war, Zuse was rather restricted in what he could do and make because of the limitations of materials and other resources, and because certain activities of German nationals were curtailed. It was not until 1950 that he could go ahead with new work. This took the form of manufacturing his own computers. Together with two friends he formed the firm Zuse KG near Bad Hersfeld, Hessen. His next computer, the Z5 was again a relay computer and it was delivered to the Leitz Optical Factory in Wetzlar in 1952. It was very much faster than his wartime machines and had greater programming facilities. Other relay computers were also built which were popular with optical manufacturers, town and country surveys and universities.

It was not until 1955 that Germans were allowed to manufacture electronic devices of the kind needed for computers. This rather hampered Zuse and German computer development as a whole. He and his firm went on to manufacture electronic machines but they were at first very much eclipsed by the British and American computers. However, the Z22 was one of the first transistorised computers to be built; it was operational in 1958. As time passed, Zuse's independent company passed gradually into other hands and in 1969 it was under the full control of Siemens AG. After many years as a busy manager, its founder was again able to take up scientific research.

During the 1960s many honours came Zuse's way: he was admitted a Doctor Honoris Causa of the Technical University of Berlin and appointed an honourary Professor of Gottingen University. Professor Zuse is still actively involved in the development of computer technology.

CHAPTER TEN

Alan Turing

FROM THE previous chapters it may seem that America and Germany were the only places where the electronic computers originated. This is far from the truth. A very independent line of computer development took place in Britain. Although the EDVAC report from the Moore School influenced engineers on both sides of the Atlantic after the Second World War, British computer development was already well under way with an impressive list of successes. Indeed, many of the firsts which had automatically been assumed to have begun with the ENIAC were, in fact, pre-empted by British machines. Although these advances were not the work of just one man, they did begin with the theoretical work of only one, and the same person played a significant role, either directly or through his influence, in several aspects of early computer development in Britain. This man was Alan **Turing**, whose theoretical notion of the concept of a general purpose computer as a logical construction gave a stimulus to the development of a practical machine in the late 1930s. His work with the creation of the ACE and Pilot ACE computers at the National Physical Laboratory and his later association with the Manchester University computer project also place him as one of the leading figures in post-war development.

Alan Turing was, by any standard, an eccentric. Many strange stories are told about him, which bear this out and also give a definite impression of a man who led a lonely life. But the solitude was, for the most part, turned into a single-mindedness which guided him to heights of genius.

Alan Mathison Turing was born at Warrington Lodge,

Alan Turing. (Photo: *By Elliot and Fry from the book Alan M. Turing by Sara Turing, Heffer, Cambridge, 1959. Courtesy also of the National Physical Laboratory.*)

Maida Vale, London on the 23rd June 1912. His father held a senior position in the Indian Civil Service. Because of this, he was frequently separated from his parents during his childhood. Only a little after his first birthday his mother rejoined her husband in India, leaving him in the care of close family friends. Although he had an elder brother, Alan was often to be found alone making discoveries about the world around him, or performing rudimentary experiments. It is said that he was slow to learn to read until he found a simple reading book and taught himself in a short time. After a little while at a private school for very young children, he was taken away by his mother because he seemed to be making little progress. A few months later he joined his brother at Hazlehurst Preparatory School. There he gained an interest in chess, which was to last throughout his life, and he joined the debating society. He was still preoccupied with his own investigations, however. In most subjects he was good, but by no means outstanding. His great failing was writing. He was a very untidy worker. Not infrequently his work was much shorter than had been anticipated by his masters. Alan often had the ability to see through a question and to write down the correct answer without any explanatory working. This facility is not always appreciated by schoolmasters! In 1926 he took the Common Entrance Examination and went on to Sherborne School.

On joining his new public school, he showed a strange mixture of eccentricity, audacity and self-reliance. The General Strike was in progress when the term began, so Alan travelled the sixty miles from his home on a bicycle, staying overnight in the best hotel in Blandford. Whether or not the individualist that was Alan enjoyed public school, with its loneliness, strange customs and intense pressure to conform, he accepted it and eventually acquitted himself well. During his early years at Sherborne he was in the habit of falling behind in his studies during mid-term, only to come out with high marks in the examinations. His thoughts may well have been on other things; he often pursued a deep investigation into topics to the detriment of the more superficial work required by his teachers. During his time at school he wrote a commentary on Einstein's book *Relativity* for the edification of his mother. As time passed, he impressed his masters with his ability in science and mathematics. In 1929 Alan took the scholarship examination for Cambridge University, but he qualified only for an exhibition. This was not thought to be good enough by either his father or himself. The following year he re-sat the examination and was awarded a full scholarship. By this time his talents had earned him the recognition at school which perhaps his personality alone could never have guaranteed him. As part of school life, Alan had acquitted himself well on the sports field; his love of running was to show itself later in a grander way when he did well in major long distance events. During his school days he had carried off all the endowed prizes for mathematics. On leaving, he chose von Neumann's book on quantum theory *Mathematische Grundlagen der Quantenmechanik* as part of one of these. Was there an omen in this?

The following term Alan went up to King's College, Cambridge. As a scholar, the recipient of a scholarship, he had some standing in the college and a lot was expected of him. Soon, however, he became involved in his private mathematical investigations again and lost ground in his normal studies to the extent that he obtained only a second class pass in the first part of his examinations. This was very soon remedied, and throughout the rest of his undergraduate studies he showed himself to be a very able mathematician. He added rowing to his hobbies and he played quite a lot of chess. In 1934 he took his final examinations and was awarded his degree with distinction. The Harold Fry Studentship was made available to him by King's College so that he could continue his studies and he returned to his college again the following October.

Throughout his life, Turing had all the benefits of an upper middle class family. There was no shortage of money, and long holidays were spent walking, climbing, boating and fishing with the rest of his family in various parts of the British Isles. Also, more ambitious visits to the continent were sometimes made with friends or with his mother. Even with all his advantages, Alan developed a reliance on his own physical effort which is rare in anyone; he would walk, run or bicycle immense distances. In later years he would often run between important meetings, and stay in hostels instead of the comfortable hotels which he would easily afford.

As a newly graduated exceptional student it was important to obtain a fellowship of his college. This was the beginning of a university teaching career at Cambridge, which would eventually give him the freedom to carry out research without having to worry too much about the more practical organisation of his life. The following March, when he was twenty-three he submitted his dissertation for a fellowship on the 'Gaussian Error Function' and was later awarded the prized appointment. The following year this work was submitted for the coveted Cambridge mathematics award, the Smith's Prize. Even before this was safely made his own, he was busy on what was to be his best known theoretical work.

To understand the purpose of this work we will have to digress a little, to the work of David Hilbert, the German mathematician who we will meet again in connection with von Neumann. Hilbert was the leader of what has become known as the 'Formalist School', which was seeking to build firm foundations for the whole subject of mathematics. The formalists believed that all mathematics problems could be solved. The proof that some problems could not be solved in a finite number of definite steps was the conclusion of Turing's famous paper entitled 'On Computable Numbers, with an Application to the Entscheidungsproblem'. (This result was not quite the same as that of the Austrian, Kurt Godel, who showed that it was impossible to decide whether the rules of arithmetic were consistent with each other and were such that they always gave mathematics which was free from contradictions. But this is another story.) The conclusion was not the important part for the theory of computers, it was the logical constructs he developed to reach this that became important. Since these are not really connected with the development of actual machines, they will be discussed at length in a later chapter. This work, even when it was first published, went some way towards establishing Turing's reputation as a mathematical logician.

In 1936 Alan Turing decided to go to America and study at the Graduate School, Princeton. For the journey he bought a secondhand sextant, and in his letters home he gave his version of the ship's position. This showed something of his desire to pursue interesting things, albeit out of the ordinary ones, for their own sake. It was a lifelong trait of his, to begin whatever he did with as basic a starting point as possible. With regard to the ship's position, a less determined person would have observed the sun and stars and corrected his initial guesses by getting a more accurate position from one of the ship's officers.

Princeton was the home of many distinguished mathematicians and scientists. It was here that he met Johnny von Neumann for the first time. Von Neumann, who had begun his own mathematical career with great investigations into the foundations of mathematics and mathematical logic, showed great interest in Turing's work on computable numbers. But it was not with von Neumann that he came to study, it was with Alonzo Church. Church was one of the foremost American logicians of the time, and his interests were very close to those of Alan. At his suggestion, Alan gave a lecture on computable numbers, but very few people attended. In contrast to his work at Cambridge, Turing's first research at Princeton was concerned with the theory of mathematical groups. It was only during his second year that he settled down to consolidate his research in mathematical logic.

Between his two years in America, Turing returned to England. Before he left Princeton he was uncertain whether to return, partly because he did not have a great affinity with life in America or its academic scene and partly because he felt his work on computable numbers had not received its just desserts. However, on the promise of a Princeton Fellowship and the stipend it entailed, and because of a genuine desire on the part of the senior members of the graduate school, he decided to return. In his second year Alan wrote his doctoral dissertation on 'Systems of Logic based on Ordinals'. This second masterpiece became somewhat more extensive than was Turing's original intention on the advice of Church. Later, this difficult work was published and it is seen as a great step in the development of a particular branch of mathematical logic. The doctorate was awarded by Princeton in May 1938, and Alan returned to England shortly afterwards. Curiously, Turing was often a little embarrassed at being addressed as 'Doctor' in England. He had a feeling that since it was an American degree, the title only counted on the far side of the Atlantic. Before he left America he gave some thought to finding a job. Although von Neumann offered him a position as his assistant, he decided to return to his native land.

Once in England, he returned to Cambridge but he was not to stay in the tranquil academic atmosphere for long. The signs of war were then very clear and no doubt the British Government, being aware of the nation's future needs, were on the lookout for able and skilled people. It hardly seems credible that an eccentric mathematical logician would have anything of practical value to offer his country in time of war. But so it was. In his paper on computable numbers, Alan had shown that he knew something of great national importance. Because of this, he found himself shanghaid into the Foreign Office and sent to work at a country house with rather extensive and hurriedly erected outbuildings. This rural manor was Bletchley Park, Buckinghamshire, the home of the Government Code and Cypher School. Turing was going to break Germany's military codes.

Even now the wartime work at Bletchley Park is surrounded with secrecy, and the information which has been released tends to be peripheral and incomplete. Much of what is known comes from descriptions given by people who worked there during the war years. A great deal of coded information was gleaned by the British from listening to the radio signals of the German forces. Much of this information was described as ULTRA because of the way it was coded. By a series of fortuitous events, the British authorities knew, even before the outbreak of war, the method of coding the ULTRA messages. An ingenious mechanical coding machine, which had been devised and was operating in Europe for ordinary commercial purposes, was adopted for military use. The principle of the machine had been used for quite a number of years, and was based on an earlier American device. These military code machines were known as ENIGMAs. The ENIGMA machines had either three or four rotos (naval codes) each of which contained the letters of the alphabet. The letters of the message to be coded were typed on the machine using a typewriter keyboard. As a letter entered the ENIGMA, it generated a letter on the first rotor, which fed a substitute letter on to the second rotor, and so on, so that a new letter was substituted three or four times for the one in the message. To make things even more secure, a plugboard of connections on the ENIGMA further altered the substitution of coded letters for the message. The receiver of the message needed to know the initial settings of the sender's machine, those of the rotors and those of the plugboard. To decode the message he simply ran the ENIGMA machine backwards.

Even with an ENIGMA machine it was extremely difficult to break the ULTRA code because there were about 10^{21} possibilities for the initial settings of the machine. These, of course, were changed frequently by the enemy, sometimes as often as three times a day. In principle, the idea was simple. But it was impossible to examine all the possible combinations that could be used to code a message, even with vast armies of people trying different combinations. However, a machine which relied on speed might succeed.

It is believed that Alan Turing first came to Bletchley Park to work on ULTRA. The one machine that least is known about seems to be the one used initially for this. At about the time of the outbreak of war, Turing put his idea of a theoretical computing machine to good use and he is believed to have played a major part in the design of the BOMBE.

These machines have been described as being contained in a keyhole shaped copper cabinet about eight feet high and a similar width at the base. This accounts for the description of these machines as 'Bronze Goddesses'. The details of their working have not yet been released, but people acquainted with them say that they sounded like the clickings of a hundred knitting needles. This description strongly suggests that they were electromechanical machines built from telephone relays, rather like the Stibnitz computers or a small version of the Aiken one. It is believed that the Goddesses were built around the time of the outbreak of war by the British Tabulating Machine Company at Letchworth.

For some time Turing was in charge of one section, Hut 8, which used these machines to crack the ULTRA messages. Together with some skilled mathematical help, the human work of the section was carried out by thirty or so Wrens.

ULTRA messages continued throughout the hostilities, apparently without the Germans suspecting the success of Hut 8 at Bletchley Park, which contributed considerably to the eventual victory of the Allies. The ease with which Bletchley Park succeeded with ULTRA, at least at times, is seen when

RAF meteorological information to bomber crews was frequently based on German Luftwaffe ULTRA weather reports. But ULTRA was the everyday way of coding messages. Certain high-level strategic information, it is believed, was coded by a much more elaborate version of the ENIGMA. This GEHEIMSCHREIBER machine was bigger and much less portable than the ENIGMA and it had ten rotors in place of the three or four of the smaller machine. Also the GEHEIMSCHREIBER further used the standard BAUDOT teleprinter code in the actual transmission of messages for operational convenience. Obviously, the Germans felt the need for two levels of code and they probably believed that their high security measures were more than enough for man or machine. How the subsequent work on code-breaking computers at Bletchley Park was concerned with the nature of the code involved, is largely a matter for conjecture. However later machines represented a considerable step forward over the 'Godesses' in speed and their development was probably stimulated by the need to attack the GEHEIMSCHREIBER codes. No doubt, they were later to be of considerable benefit in decoding the ULTRA messages.

The origin of the new machines came about when Professor M. H. A. **Newman** joined Bletchley Park from Cambridge. Newman had been one of Turing's lecturers and is even believed to have given him the idea for the famous paper on computable numbers. Cryptanalysis, the breaking of codes, did not, at first, seem to be Newman's forte and he considered leaving until he saw that machines could be applied to his work. This resulted in the setting up of a new section in Hut F to work on this. Soon, as in the haste of war, the Post Office Research Station at Dollis Hill and the Telecommunications Research Establishment, TRE (which was deeply concerned in the development of radar) became involved, each contributing a part with Turing in frequent contact with the teams. The result was the HEATH ROBINSON, a machine not unlike the weird sealing wax and string creations of its cartoonist namesake. The two parts of the new code breaker were put together at Bletchley park and ROBINSON became operational in April 1943.

The HEATH ROBINSON was designed to read and compare the characters punched on two paper tapes. It was intended to read these photoelectrically at a rate of about 2,000 per second, but often it was much slower because the tapes had a tendency to break. This machine had about 50 valves and presumably a great amount of associated circuitry and many electromagnetic relays. The output was a fairly primitive line printer. In practice it did not work well, frequently breaking down and even smouldering as the high-speed drives rubbed against paper tape which had stuck and it is believed that relatively little useful information was initially obtained. There were, however, further machines built in this series which included the PETER ROBINSON and the ROBINSON & CLEAVER. Also, even when the work had been superseded by a new series of machines, a SUPER ROBINSON was built.

It is believed that Turing played a large role in the development of HEATH ROBINSON, together with Newman, whose idea it was, and C. E. **Wynn-Williams** and T. H. Flowers, the leaders of the engineering. Although Flowers joined the ROBINSON project after its initiation, he played the major engineering role in what was to come.

T. H. **Flowers** was in charge of the switch group at the Post Office Research Station. He had served his apprenticeship at Woolwich Arsenal and then went to Dollis Hill as a probationary engineer in 1930. He had worked on long distance signalling and the transmitting of control signals. The experience he gained in the latter might well have helped him considerably with his work for Bletchley Park. Later, he gained some knowledge of the Bush differential analyser at Manchester. After the start of the war he became involved with a number of special projects, including electromechanical and electronic devices with very new and special military purposes.

Flowers came to play a significant part in the development of the ROBINSONS, but when he saw that they were not really equal to their task he attempted to get backing from the authorities at Bletchley Park to build an improved version. This backing was not at first forthcoming, so he and his team began the design of the new machine alone. When the prototype COLOSSUS, as the new machine was called, was demonstrated, it proved to be just what was required. Its speed, success rate and reliability further endeared it to the code breakers. The first COLOSSUS had about 1,500 valves. One of the two tapes of the ROBINSONS had been replaced by electronic circuitry, and so one of the major problems of keeping the two tapes synchronised had been overcome. The output was an electric typewriter.

The reliability of thermionic valves had caused opposition at first to Flower's project, especially since a design incorporating so many was, at that time untried anywhere. He overcame the problem by intending that the COLOSSUS should remain switched on the whole time, as valves tend to fail shortly after they become conducting and are likely to have their lives shortened by the shocks due to heating and cooling from intermittent rather than continuous activity.

The prototype COLOSSUS went into operation during December 1943. This places it as probably the world's first operational computer. It utilised binary arithmetic and performed Boolean logic operations (see later); also it was capable of altering its mode of operation depending on the results it achieved. The operator was an integral part of the code processing system since, while the COLOSSUS was operating, he scanned the output and altered the circuits via a plugboard to effect different code breaking hypotheses and eventually centred on the correct technique. The prototype machine was capable of reading 5,000 characters per second.

When the Mark 1 (prototype) worked so well, Flowers enquired as to whether more were required. He was met with a noncommittal answer, but he again set about preparing an improved version. As in all the best tales of wartime production, when he was asked the following March to make more COLOSSI he was given too short a time, three were needed for the 1st June 1944. One was ready and waiting with literally minutes to spare. The others followed shortly afterwards. In all, about ten Mark 2 COLOSSI were made. Each one was slightly different and somewhat improved from the previous one. Generally, they had about 2,500 valves and operated five parallel sets of character reading circuits which meant that they were capable of reading 25,000 characters per second. These machines represent a truly magnificent achievement and must have played a considerable part in the British and American success towards the end of the war.

Shortly after the hostilities ceased, a number of electronics experts and specialists in the embryonic science of computer design saw the COLOSSI at Bletchley Park and were suitably impressed. This visit, like so much concerned with this aspect of computer development, was top secret. What eventually became of the BOMBES, the ROBINSONS and the CO-LOSSI is still secret. Let us hope, however, that they have not all been destroyed and that one day we will be able to inspect them in museums. In the 1970s there was a release of some photographs and a description of the COLOSSI, and later, some ULTRA messages were made public. The description of the COLOSSI credits Newman with the idea for the machine, Flowers for its construction and development and Turing for the underlying theory. For their services to Britain, Turing was awarded the OBE and Flowers the MBE.

When the BOMBES first proved successful, their design was passed to the Americans, who presumably adopted and possibly improved it. There are also probably American cryptanalytic machines which are still secret, so it could well be some time before we know the whole story. Alan Turing is known to have visited the United States at least once, and possibly twice during the war. It is not, however, thought that it had to do with the BOMBE, which was a machine he was closely involved with, but that it concerned work on the atomic bomb. However, he is not mentioned by any of the authors who have written about the development of this weapon. In America he is said to have visited von Neumann, whom he knew from his days at Princeton. Although the legend says that the two great men sorted out the postwar development of computers between them, there now seems to be very little evidence that the meeting ever took place.

Turing's duties at Bletchley Park changed at least once. He left Hut 8 and went to work at something else. It is reported that he developed a new aspect of statistical theory during this time, but that it was then secret and the same results have, in postwar years, been discovered by and credited to others. Only recently an article has been published which described the extent and worth of his wartime statistical research.

His eccentricities did not disappear during these wartime exploits, and there are a good many tales about him. Alan is reputed to have used his gas mask for the eminently practical purpose of preventing the onset of hay fever. Each morning he cycled to work at Bletchley Park. The bicycle he used is the centre of a story. There was a broken cog on one of the sprocket wheels which caused the chain to come off every so many revolutions of the pedals. Instead of having his means of transport repaired, he preferred to count the number of strokes of the pedals and then take his own temporary remedial action just in the nick of time. It is with a certain sympathy that I view his habit of fastening his tea mug to a radiator with a padlock and chain. A person is in for an annoying experience when such an important article goes missing, but this totally in-character method was taking things a little far, even in those desperate days.

Perhaps the most fascinating story of this time happened shortly after the start of the war, when he withdrew a considerable sum of money from the bank. He firmly believed, as no doubt did many other people, that if Germany should win the war, then the money in bank accounts would be either frozen, confiscated or worthless. With his cash he bought two large silver ingots; rare metal, like stamps and precious stones, is always negotiable currency. He then buried the ingots for the duration of the war. When things again returned to normal, he set out to where he thought he had buried his treasure armed with an inadequate sketch map and his own home made metal detector. Unfortunately, neither of these aids was of any use and he was unable to retrieve his precious metal.

At Bletchley Park Turing was respected by all, even many senior people were in awe of him. However, his manner and eccentricities were such that many people found him offputting. With his friends he played chess. Even though he was a keen and experienced player, he was not in the same league as many of the Bletchley Park people, who included some masters among their number, and did not make the team. His other off-duty interest was talking about the possible development of the electronic computer and what tasks it could perform. One of his pet ideas, which he did develop after the war, was the notion of computers playing chess.

When the workers at Bletchley Park returned to their normal occupations, Alan wanted to continue his work on computers. The building of these machines was now an important aspect of the postwar development of mathematics, Alan and many others had learned about the ENIAC and the plans for the EDVAC. No doubt it was with a great deal of difficulty that many people who knew of the Bletchley Park machines kept this knowledge to themselves when visiting the Moore School of Electrical Engineering at the University of Pennsylvania shortly after the war. Also a summer school on American computer development was held there in 1946 which did much to disseminate the EDVAC concept, and it was from this that M.V. Wilkes began his work on the Cambridge EDSAC, a machine very similar in concept and much earlier in operation than the EDVAC. Computer development was very much in the air, but there were two aspects, the public American developments and the secret British work.

When Alan was given the opportunity of joining the National Physical Laboratory (NPL) to work on the design of a computer, he had no desire to return to academic life. The NPL created a mathematics division with Alan Turing as a senior principal scientific officer in charge of the electronics section. There were also sections concerned with punched card processing, statistics and the differential analyser. Turing's plan was to build a general purpose computer, the Automatic Computing Engine (ACE). This was given considerable support initially by the authorities as they knew of the wartime achievements and there was a desire for a national computing facility for scientists and engineers.

Turing concerned himself mainly with the logical design and the means of programming the proposed machine. In 1945 he prepared a very lengthy report on the design of computers which came after von Neumann's EDVAC document, but went further and deeper, so that it was more like the later report of the Americans concerning the IAS machine (see the chapter on von Neumann.) He even gave some time to researching the mathematical methods which would be needed when the new machine was in action. Turing was not an engineer and his understanding of large-scale electronic circuitry was not in the same class as the men at Dollis Hill and the TRE. It was intended that outside help would be found for this part of the work, but many of the engineers capable of participating were involved with other work. Flowers was working on the postwar telephone network. The Post Office team, now led by A. W. M. Coombes who had also been a senior member of the COLOSSUS design team, went on to build a large defence computer MOSAIC (Ministry of Supply Automatic Integrator and Computer) which was a delay line machine used initially to process radar tracking data. The TRE were working on their own TREAC (Telecommunications Research Establishment Automatic Computer) which was a parallel machine with cathode ray tube stores. MOSAIC went into operation in 1952 and TREAC in 1954 Certainly these two machines owe a lot to the work on the COLOSSI. (Indeed the American pioneers were very surprised when Britain was able to begin such an ambitious, large-scale project so early).

With regard to ACE there was considerable progress on paper but no signs of hardware construction. Also Turing kept revising his designs. When H. D. Huskey, who had worked on the ENIAC, arrived at the NPL he suggested that a small-scale machine should be made that just demonstrated the possibilities intended for the ACE. However, Turing was rather disheartened at the lack of progress and decided to return to his college at Cambridge, where he was still a fellow, for a sabbatical year. When he came back to the NPL in May 1948, he felt that things had not improved sufficiently to induce him to stay. So before the completion of even the pilot ACE he accepted an offer to join his old friend M.H.A. Newman, now professor of mathematics at the University of Manchester.

The Pilot ACE was eventually completed and it came into operation in May 1950. It was very much Turing's conception, although it was assembled by others. Turing was a great believer in the programmer doing as much work as possible, with the result that the Pilot ACE was a very powerful, but unconventional machine which was very difficult to program. It had delay line storage, about 800 valves and punched card input and output. From even its initial demonstration, it worked very well. In fact, its success was so great that an engineering production model called DEUCE was produced by the English Electric Company. Pilot ACE worked at the NPL until about 1958 when it became an exhibit at the Science Museum, South Kensington.

The intended ACE was eventually operating in 1957. By

this time it was based on a number of ideas which had been superceded and its delay lines were inferior to the then modern core storage. These machines, especially the Pilot ACE were not really direct antecedents of modern machines. Turing's ideas as they materialised in hardware, were, perhaps, too economical on machinery and too demanding on the operator, and, even though DEUCE was a commercial development of Pilot ACE many of the design concepts it embodied were later abandoned.

Turing went to Manchester University in September 1948 to become Reader in Mathematics in the department headed by M. A. H. Newman. He was also appointed Deputy Director of the Computing Machine Laboratory. Already this laboratory had had an important initial success. On the 21st June 1948 a very small prototype computer using a cathode ray tube store, operated its first program. This is believed to be the world's first stored program computer to operate. Turing had come into a team with considerable engineering expertise led by F. C. Williams and with Tom Kilburn as a senior member.

F. C. **Williams** had been appointed to the chair of electrotechnics in December 1946. Frederick Calland Williams was born at Romily near Stockport on the 26th June 1911. After being educated at Stockport Grammar School he entered Manchester University with a scholarship in 1929 and graduated in 1932. The following year he was awarded an MSc. For a short period he worked for the Metropolitan-Vickers Electrical Company until he was awarded a Ferranti Scholarship of the Institution of Electrical Engineers. This allowed him to carry out research into circuit and valve noise at the University of Oxford. For this work he was awarded a doctorate in 1936. The same year he returned to Manchester University as an assistant lecturer. During the war years he worked at the TRE on the development of radar and on feedback systems known as servomechanisms. After the hostilities ended he visited the MIT where he learned of the first attempts to use 'iconoscopes' (television camera tubes) as storage devices for computers. He followed up this idea and made the cathode ray tube storage systems which have already been mentioned. In deference to his success, these are often known as Williams' Tubes, and because of their nature, they allowed parallel stores to be built and parallel computers to be developed. Delay lines were sequential access memories. Also they were ordinary television tubes which were cheap and worked simply by storing information as spots on a phosphorescent screen. As the images deteriorated they were renewed by new electrical impulses. In the 1950s his interest in electronic computers waned and he turned his attention to electrical machines and the automatic transmission mechanisms for motor cars. For his achievements both during and after the war he was elected a Fellow of the Royal Society in 1950 and received a knighthood in 1976. Sir F. C. Williams died on the 11th August 1977.

Before leaving Williams it is important to point out his part in another aspect of computer development. As was mentioned in the chapter on Vannevar Bush, the differential analyser was a mechanical computer which was succeeded in postwar years by the electronic analogue computer. It was during his war work that Williams designed the basic circuitry for the operational amplifier, the main type of electronic device which makes up these computers.

Alan Turing could not, of course, match the electrical skills of Williams and so the problem which had dogged him at the NPL became inverted. Instead of striving for knowledge and experience of electronics in the people around him, he was now unable to keep up with that which was present. Because of this, he contributed very little to the design of the Manchester computers. That which he did contribute directly was concerned with the input and output mechanisms.

In October 1949, a much larger computer was operating, which became known as the Mark 1 or MADM (Manchester Automatic Digital Machine). Turing wrote the operating manual for his computer and also developed techniques of programming. An engineered version of this machine was built for the University by Ferranti Ltd. A further nine modified versions of the Ferranti Mark I and Mark 1* were made and supplied to various firms and institutions throughout the world. From 1951 the Williams' team developed a Mark II computer which was eventually manufactured by Ferranti as the Mercury. Later in the same line of development came the Atlas transistorised computer.

As time passed, Turing retreated from the active development of the actual machines and worked on programming and the application of mathematics to electronic computation in the form of numerical analysis. He continued his interest in programming computers to play chess and became rather preoccupied with the process which took place inside the computer generally. Was this intelligence? Could machines ever become capable of intelligent thought? We shall see the conclusions he came to in the next chapter.

In 1951 he was elected a Fellow of the Royal Society, the greatest honour that can be bestowed on a British scientist. His election was proposed by his friend and senior colleague at Manchester, M. H. A. Newman. The person who seconded his election was Bertrand Russell, one of the foremost mathematical logicians of all time. He is remembered for his famous logical work *Principia Mathematica*, but he also had a considerable reputation as a twentieth century philosopher and he has contributed significantly to many areas of this subject.

Alan's interests later turned to scientific investigation. His haphazard methods for chemistry experiments came to the fore again. In the house which he bought in Manchester, he set up a small laboratory in which to carry out his witch's brew chemistry. He believed very much in being self-sufficient in all things, starting always at the beginning, whether in computers, mathematics or chemistry. Many of his experiments were attempts to make common household and other chemical products from their starting points. Turing must have spent many hours in these pursuits and gained considerable personal satisfaction, since he carried out all manner of experiments in the rather innocent and undisciplined way which was more appropriate to an intelligent small boy with an over-sized chemistry set. This was in direct contrast to another chemical investigation he carried out at a theoretical level. He became interested in systems where chemicals were being synthesised, decomposed and carried away, all at the same time. This set up was further complicated since it took place as part of the biochemistry of a living creature. He believed these processes of reaction and diffusion could produce chemical waves which led to the formation of patterns and shapes. One of his pet examples for explaining what he was doing was to say that it explained the black and brown patches on cows.

These chemical systems which underlie biological morpho-genesis can be described precisely only in terms of mathematics. The mathematical models needed are very hard to put together and very much more difficult to solve when more than two chemical reactions are involved. Indeed, they involved complicated partial differential equations. The enormous role these equations play in describing scientific processes and their importance as motivating factor in the development of the electronic computer has already been mentioned. Turing took the opportunity of using the Manchester computer to solve these equations. The results were promising but all but the simplest biological systems yielded sets of equations which were beyond even the computational resources at his disposal.

His work on biological chemistry was published in the influential *Philosophical Transactions of the Royal Society B* in 1952. It was recognised as an important development in biology and is mentioned even today. Progress since this time has not, however, been great because of both the mathematical and computational difficulties and because, perhaps, biologists have had much more exciting things to do.

For his chemical experiments, Turing kept a bottle of the very poisonous potassium cyanide. He used this chemical, like many others, in a very careless way. On the 8th June 1954, he was found dead in his bed, his death caused by cyanide poisoning. Whether this was self-administered or not can never be known. The coroner's verdict was suicide, but his mother and some of his friends felt that he had so many exciting things in his life and had made so many future plans that this was very unlikely.

Alan Turing, because of his famous theoretical work of 1936 on computable numbers, can claim to be one of the fathers of the general purpose computer. Within one and a half decades he made further enormous contributions to a practical machine which then was passed by. The development of the computer was so rapid that it demanded a multitude of traditional and new skills from anyone who was going to remain its complete master. Few, if any, of the pioneers were able to remain masters of all the necessary engineering and software developments and mathematics after this time. The next generation were computer developers, each a specialist in his own field. Turing, as we have seen, found his influence on computer development diminish, initially at the NPL and later at Manchester University; this must have been a great disappointment to him.

CHAPTER ELEVEN

John von Neumann

DEVELOPMENTS in the computer came about in many cases, as we have seen, in response to the needs of engineers and scientists. That their needs were magnified by the hostilities of the Second World War is not surprising, because technology played a large part in the development of weapons. The midwives at the birth of the electronic computer were engineers and physicists working under the frenetic circumstances of a world in turmoil. How long it would have taken for it to emerge under calmer circumstances can never be known, but there was no real reason why it could not have been developed a decade earlier. It so often seems that human, social and cultural unease is productive, whereas a calm and tranquil existence, either of an individual or a society, produces an attenuated will to make progress. However, what cannot emerge during frantic activity under pressure of time and circumstance is a smooth concept in which all the major problems have either been solved or displaced. Perhaps in a time of peace a more polished and cheaper machine (expense is relatively easy to justify during a war) would have emerged in place of the ENIAC. But this is doubtful since crude hypotheses invariably preceed more refined ones. What is fairly certain at the time in which the ENIAC was under construction, is that computers were machines being developed by engineers and physicists. Although these people were of considerable mathematical ability, no real front-rank mathematician had become involved. The first person of such stature was John **von Neumann**. Von Neumann came at the right time

John von Neumann beside the Princeton Institute for Advanced Study computer. (Photo: *Courtesy of the Institute for Advanced Study, Princeton, New Jersey.*)

to give the mathematician's insight into the process of changing a workable machine into an efficient one.

John (Janos) Louis Neumann was born in Budapest on 28th December 1903. Budapest was then the second city of the Austro-Hungarian Empire and the centre of wealthy business and banking interests. Von Neumann was born into a cultured and comfortably off family which derived its success from its commercial and banking activities. In Hungarian, Janos was contracted to Janci and it was later anglicised to Johnny, the name by which he was universally known to his friends. Johnny's father, Max, was a successful banker who was ennobled by the Emperor and given the Hungarian title 'Margattai'. This was not quite the high honor it might seem, since the Empire was inclined to use such titles as a kind of currency; it bought high favours with them or simply sold them for cash. It was for the former reason that such an honour was given to Max Neumann in 1913; he was to use his influence to help to protect the financial interests of Hungary. When Johnny later went to study and work in Germany, he showed his family's ennoblement by using the aristocratic 'von'.

During his early childhood he was taught by a German governess. He thus learned German as well as Hungarian. Reading and calculating were his favourite activities. At the age of ten he began to attend the Lutheran Gymnasium in the city. His abilities were prodigious. His knowledge of languages was considerable, especially the classical ones of Latin and Greek around which the curriculum of the school revolved. After only a few months his mathematics teacher felt that he was forced to bring the young Janci's ability in the subject to the attention of his father. It was not that Ladislas Ratz, his mathematics master, was unwilling to teach the boy, it was that this was not in his best interests. Janci was obvuously an exceptionally-gifted mathematician who required special training. As a result of this, Max Neumann, through his contacts at the University of Budapest found Michael Fekete, a young and able mathematician, to tutor his son.

Through Fekete, Janci became acquainted with the mathematics and mathematicians of the time. He thus had an early and direct entry into the higher reaches of the subject. His progress was such that before he left the gymnasium he was showing his mettle as a research mathematician with his first paper, a collaboration with Fekete, written when he was only eighteen. When he passed the 'matura' and left school in 1921, he was considered to have great talent and to show considerable promise.

His school days, however, could never have been tranquil. In 1914, the year he began school, the political currents which had long been flowing in Hungary and the world at large, erupted into the Great War. The effects on Budapest were disastrous; it was left as the capital of a small state which had been ruined in the conflict. It is fortunate that bankers are always needed, and the von Neumann family suffered less than most. In the wake of the war, the communists were active in Hungary and in March 1919, led by Bela Kun, they formed a coalition government with the Social Democrats. Soon the position of the rich was changed. Von Neumann was prevented from doing his work at the bank and groups of leather-jacketed toughs and ex-criminals, known as 'Lenin Boys' roamed the streets beating up and harassing the rich. The situation was sufficiently frightening to send the von Neumanns off in retreat to Austria. Five months later the communists were displaced. The revenge taken by the right wing government that was then formed, was no less dramatic and terrible, but this time the von Neumanns were seen to be on the right side and were safe.

In 1921 Johnny went to university, or rather universities; three of them. He enrolled at the University of Budapest to study mathematics but he spent very little time there. Instead, he spent most of his time between 1921–23 at the University of Berlin, where he attended the lectures given by the famous Albert Einstein, world renowned for his theories of relativity, and other leading mathematicians of the time. From 1923 he also spent time at the Swiss Federal Technical University (Eidgenössische Technische Hochschule) in Zurich, where he gained a first degree in chemistry in 1925. Throughout his academic wanderings he kept in touch with the University of Budapest and returned at the appropriate times to take his examinations. These he passed with very high marks without having attended the courses on which they were based. However, he abandoned his travels in 1925 to write the thesis for his doctorate, which was awarded the following year.

Long before any of his courses of study were drawing to a

close, he embarked on a new academic adventure. One of his professors at Berlin, Erhard Schmidt, had been a student of the foremost mathematician of the first part of the twentieth century, David Hilbert. Schmidt lectured on Hilbert's discoveries and gave von Neumann an appetite for more of the same material. So von Neumann was to spend time at the mathematics department of the University of Göttingen. Göttingen was world-renowned for its mathematical research; some even said it was 'the centre of the mathematical universe'. This reputation stemmed from the presence of David Hilbert and Feliz Klein as professors, and from a whole host of minor stars who were later to achieve greatness. By 1924, when von Neumann was still only twenty-one and technically an undergraduate, he spent long hours closeted with Hilbert in his study or in his garden, where he preferred to work on fine days. There is no doubt that the great master, Hilbert, had much to offer the younger man, but this was a partnership with von Neumann contributing profound ideas.

Much of their work together concerned the foundations of mathematics and the theory of sets. The sets they were concerned with are the same collections of members which we talk about at school, but the theory was much more advanced. Part of von Neumann's work was an extension of that of the founder of set theory, Georg Cantor, and the rest was concerned with trying to find a basis for the theory which avoided the paradoxes that the mathematical logicians, notably Bertrand Russell, had discovered. Von Neumann published several important papers on set theory, and also his doctorate was awarded for work on this topic.

During the 1920s the quantum theory of the atom was the major preoccupation of physicists, with new developments being reported almost daily. This theory is a complex of physical ideas, but the central notion is that the energy changes between atomic particles occur in multiples of certain fixed amounts, known as quanta. Hilbert had a keen interest in theoretical physics and was very much concerned with the background to the theory. He also attempted to achieve a set of basic notions, or axioms, for physics. Sets of axioms such as those for geometry or groups, were common in mathematics, but physics proved more intractable. Von Neumann was influenced by Hilbert's idea and set out to find an axiomatic basis for quantum mechanics. It was the embodiment of his researches in his book *Mathematische Grundlagen der Quantenmechanik*, in English *Mathematical Foundations of Quantum Mechanics*, which was the first and only major achievement in the axiomatisation of physics. It was also the same work which Alan Turing accepted as a school prize.

Following the award of his doctorate, von Neumann obtained a position as Privatdozent at the University of Berlin. This was an appointment as recognised, but unpaid, lecturer; such payment as there was came directly from the students. Von Neumann had no worry about money since his family's financial resources guaranteed his independence, so he did not have to concern himself about attracting large numbers of students to his courses. However, there were many 'dozents' and very few professors, and promotion was likely to be slow and uncertain, even for a mathematician of his ability. Perhaps it was with this in mind that he successfully completed his studies in chemistry; the German chemical industry was large and progressive and could guarantee able people lucrative employment. During his three years in Berlin as a lecturer, von Neumann enjoyed the delights of the city. He loved company and spent many of his evenings at parties or nightclubs. During the day he worked hard and achieved many new results in mathematics. Much of his research still concerned David Hilbert and others from Gottingen. Hilbert was known to be slow to understand things; von Neumann on the other hand was lightning fast. He was able to perform long calculations at great speed in his head. This was to be a great help later in his life; it was also a minor source of irritation to those who worked with him. There are well-known stories of von Neumann producing in seconds the answers to problems which others had struggled over for hours. He also said that he felt that a mathematician's powers decline after the age of twenty-six, this age limit was, however, raised as he got older.

His mathematical achievements in Berlin were considerable. He continued his work on sets and quantum mechanics and also ventured into other areas. In the mathematics underlying certain games, known, not surprisingly as game theory, he proved an important result, the minimax theorem. This was a major development in a young branch of mathematics which was to become important in economic behaviour and the representation of human affairs. To recount another development, it is again necessary to return to the life of David Hilbert. In 1900, Hilbert, being arguably the world's greatest mathematician, was asked to give a major address at the International Mathematical Congress in Paris. In this he outlined twenty-three problems whose solution he thought would stimulate mathematical research in the twentieth century. Needless to say, these were deep problems which were destined to occupy the thoughts of successive great mathematicians. Even now only a few of them have been solved completely. The mathematicians who have achieved this distinction will be remembered for a long time. Von Neumann was able to partially solve the fifth problem, which is concerned with a deep and highly abstract area of mathematics known as the theory of continuous groups.

In 1929 von Neumann moved briefly to the University of Hamburg. He was still a 'dozent, but his work had been noticed much further afield than Hungary and Germany. Through a very large grant, Princeton University was able to expand its science faculty and von Neumann and another famous Hungarian, Eugene Wigner, were invited to become visiting professors. Wigner, a distinguished physicist who was one year above von Neumann in the Lutheran Gymnasium in Budapest, and a one time assistant to David Hilbert, was later to work on the Manhattan Project. Before leaving for America in 1930, von Neumann married Mariette Koeves, the daughter of an old family friend from Budapest. Because of the recent death of his father he had to return to Europe from time to time to look after his family's affairs, so he arranged to spend the winters at Princeton and the summer semesters at the University of Berlin.

From 1933, however, he became a permanent professor at the Institute of Advanced Study at Princeton. Einstein and a number of other distinguished mathematicians also belonged to this. The Institute's professors enjoyed the highest academic salaries in America; and the Institute was a haven for some of the world's greatest mathematical talent. Von Neumann was thus established as one of the foremost mathematicians in the world.

He was happy and comfortable in America. The von Neumann household had a very active social life; large parties with lots of guests, many from the University and the Institute, were given frequently. Although he enjoyed this rich life and was well known for telling funny stories, he would frequently sneak away to his study for hours during these parties to work on problems that were bothering him. His energy, lightning-fast brain and stature as a mathematician made Johnny von Neumann a very important academic in America. His love of high living and socialising did much to help him be noticed at a level and in a country where this is most important.

In 1935 von Neumann's daughter Marina was born; later she went on to become a distinguished economist. But von Neumann's life was not without its crises, and two years later his marriage ended in divorce. This state was not to last for long and in 1938, on a summer visit to Budapest, he married Klara Dan. Klari, as she was known, was destined to become something of a pioneer of computing in her own right by developing a high standard of programming in the days when this was a very difficult, highly-skilled and intricate process.

To recount even the high points of von Neumann's successes in mathematics during the 1930s would take us into deep and abstract areas of the subject. The one topic which began to interest him more and more as that decade progressed was hydrodynamics. The mathematics underlying this involved, once again, partial differential equations. The very nature of many of the equations which he encountered was perplexing to say the least. Even a great mathematician could only solve, in closed form, a few of the simpler ones. His knowledge in this area, however, was second to none. And since the subject of hydrodynamics embraces the motion of ships, aeroplanes, shells and similar missiles and the blast waves caused by ex-plosions, von Neumann was destined to play a large part in the development of weapons during the Second World War.

In 1940 he was appointed a member of the Scientitic Advis-ory Committee to the Ballistics Research Laboratory at Aber-deen Proving Ground, and when the Manhattan Project to make the atomic bomb started in 1943, he became a consultant member of the team, spending much of his time at the labor-atories at Los Alamos in New Mexico. One of the main concerns during the development of the atomic bomb was that it would work completely and not blow itself to pieces before it got properly started. The bomb works on the principle that a suitable mass of fissile material, uranium 235 or plutonium, emits neutrons which in their paths to the outside of the metal dislodge more neutrons; a chain reaction being started as the number of neutrons increases extremely rapidly. The aim was to have a mass below the limit at which the neutrons behave this way and convert it quickly into a critical mass by adding a further mass of fissile material, or by making the original material smaller and more dense. The second method became the most important one, but to make it work properly, it was necessary that a completely symmetrical explosion compress a sphere of fissile material. The design of the explosive charges and the prediction of the shock waves they would induce led, yet again, to calculations involving partial differential equations. So for much of the war von Neumann was concerned with these equations and the lengthy methods of solving them by numerical methods which involved thousands of arithmetic multiplications.

During the time of war secrecy is paramount, and workers on different projects in the same building were normally forbidden to discuss their work. As a result of this, news of new ventures tended to travel slowly even among those who were allowed to be privy to the work. So it was that von Neumann, a consultant for the Ballistics Research Laboratory, did not learn about the real nature of the ENIAC until the summer of 1944. Herman Goldstine was waiting in Aberdeen Railway Station shortly after being released from a lengthy stay in hospital suffering from viral hepatitis, when he saw von Neumann. He introduced himself and soon got into a friendly conversation with him in which he mentioned his work on the computer. Von Neumann's interest was aroused immediately and he made arrangements to visit the Moore School.

When von Neumann arrived at Pennsylvania, the tests on the provisional design of the ENIAC equipment were under way and the design concept of this computer was effectively complete. Von Neumann's first question about the machine concerned the nature of its logical design. Generally the great man's concern with computers was to revolve around the logical conception of the computer. The electronic construction of the machine was really the province of electrical engineers, but this certainly did not mean that von Neumann was neither knowledgeable about nor interested in the electronic design; he was.

Von Neumann joined Mauchly and Eckert in time to see the ENIAC completed and to organise the problems it would first tackle. He then helped to plan the original concept of its successor, the EDVAC (Electronic Discrete Variable Computer). However, it is important to remember that Mauchly and Eckert had designed and built the ENIAC and had very definite ideas and knowledge of its shortcomings, and hence they felt very strongly about what the design of the EDVAC should accomplish. Von Neumann contributed fully in the EDVAC discussions from that time, and through his considerable insight he contributed to the logical nature of the design. ENIAC was by any standards, a rather haphazardly organised piece of equipment. Its control was decentralised; a switch had to be operated here, and another 30 feet away, wires crossed the floor and large panels of switches had to be set by hand and moved from one place to another. The memory was very inadequate, the number of valves was excessively large, bringing with it huge problems concerning the reliability of the system and a large amount of electricity was consumed. It was now felt important to produce an organised design which would be simpler amd more economical to use.

In a document *First Draft of a Report on the EDVAC*, von Neumann outlined the principles for a very high-speed, automatic digital computing system. This set of principles was a massive step forward for computer design in one sense: it laid out systematically the basis of computer organisation. In another sense we will recognise it as stating the obvious, even if it does this in a highly technical way. It is worth remembering that many of the other pioneers had ideas about the organisation of a computer, especially Babbage, so in some ways their earlier work is, perhaps unknowingly, embodied in this report. Although the article was written by von Neumann, it contains some work discussed before he became involved at the Moore School and it is, therefore, a report with Mauchly and Eckert as well as himself.

After an introduction, he outlines the main components of a computer:

    1 That it should contain a unit for performing the oper-

ations of $+$, $-$, $\times$, $\div$ and possibly many other operations. He considered the central arithmetic unit CA the first specific part of the computer.

2 A central control unit CC for the logical control of the machine.

3 A memory device M which contains not only data and partial results, but also the instructions for working through a calculation.

(Von Neumann likened the three parts CA, CC together called C ((now the CPU central processing unit)) and M to a part of the human nervous system. He then said that this must make contact with some outside recording medium, called R.)

4 An input device which transfers information from R and C and M.

5 An output device O which transfers numerical information into R.

Thus we have the common parts of the modern computer: arithmetic unit, control unit, memory and input and output devices.

The rest of the report extols the virtues of the binary system over those of the denary system for the arithmetic unit, and the way in which arithmetic operations are to be carried out. In the ENIAC, many operations were carried out simultaneously, that is in parallel with each other. Although it was known that much could be gained by this method, it was felt at the time and suggested in the report that operations should not be performed simultaneously. In other words, the EDVAC was to be a serial computer, one operation being performed after the other. This was intended to make the design of the EDVAC as simple as possible.

From the engineering point of view there was a suggestion for using the cathode ray tube as a storage device, to form part of the memory. Another idea was to identify numbers in the machine by making their first digit zero and to identify instructions by making the first digit one. (Remember, everything in the machine was to be represented by pulses of electricity which indicated the zeros or ones of a binary machine code).

The planning of the EDVAC was taking place amid the

high activity surrounding the completion and operation of the ENIAC. However, as the war ended the pressure on the team at all levels eased. As well as uncertainty about the next development in computers, there was concern about two other things. First, what members of the team were going to do now that they could be released from their government and military activities? Second, what were the credits, financial and otherwise, that were going to come from the development of the computer, and who were going to get them? This second question was the most far reaching since it governed the response of various scientists to the first. Many arguments and much consternation surrounded these. Indeed, there has been a considerable amount of litigation surrounding the origin and development of the electronic computer. This is not the place to go into it since not only work on the ENIAC and EDVAC, but that of Atanasoff and many other pioneers has been involved in many instances of legal action. The direct effect on von Neumann, Mauchly and Eckert was that the former returned to the Institute of Advanced Study and the other two set about forming the first commercial enterprise to build computers. All three were rather tired of the Moore School, and Mauchly and Eckert felt that von Neumann had been reluctant to credit them with their part in the EDVAC design. The result was that the EDVAC was eventually finished after modification by others at the Moore School in 1951, long after other machines based on its original design were completed elsewhere. This was also to be the end of the School's participation in the pioneering of large-scale computer projects.

When von Neumann returned to Princeton, there was a considerable state of flux in the academic world as well as in the new area of computer building. He had been one of the world's leading mathematicians, now he was a strong power in the administration of the government's military and scientific establishment. His connection with Los Alamos and with the Army and Navy Ordnance sections placed him in a strong position to get money for a computer, especially if it could be shown to have military applications. However, it was not quite as easy as might have been expected to get a computer project started at the Institute of Advanced Study. There were no workshops or laboratories, and there was no tradition of anything except quiet, contemplative paper and pencil research. Grants which von Neumann expected to be forthcoming from the great American institutions and foundations did not materialise. But the military eventually came forward with financial aid; part of the bargain struck was to develop the use of the computer as a tool in weather forecasting. This was no great difficulty, since the meteorological, predictions that were envisaged involved the solution of partial differential equations.

In the project for the IAS machine, or the von Neumann machine as it became known, von Neumann was appointed director with Herman Goldstine deputy director and Julian Bigelow as chief engineer. The last appointment had originally been intended for Eckert, but he preferred to go his own way.

It must be remembered that, in effect, von Neumann did not participate in the actual construction of the EDVAC, so his ideas for the machine were part of the raw material for the IAS computer. In the meantime, of course, these advanced and changed and the von Neumann machine benefited from its creators' extra and second thoughts and from the experience already gleaned on the ENIAC. The type of work for which a computer was thought useful was also a developing field, problems in hydrodynamics, quantum theory, stellar structure and meteorology could now be attempted, when previously attempts would have been extremely lengthy and utterly futile. In particular, the IAS machine benefited from von Neuman's thoughts on logical theory. It had greater efficiency of design and circuitry than the earlier machines. There was, however, a change of mind by von Neumann on the serial mode, the new computer was to be parallel machine. Multiplication was to be carried out by continued addition, that is, performing a binary calculation such as 5×32, by $32 + 32 + 32 + 32$. Division was to be carried out by repeated subtraction. The memory, which will be discussed in more detail later, was to contain both the data and the instructions for its processing. Also the instructions for the computation itself which were stored in the memory, were to be capable of modification as the program progressed.

Much of the design of the machine revolved around the convenient ways of handling problems; electronics was by now the slave and not the master in the design of the computer.

Von Neumann's new thoughts on machine design and the preparation of problems for computation were written up in a lengthy report issued in four parts and published during 1946 and 1947. The first part was called *Preliminary Discussion of the Logical Design of an Electronic Computing Instrument* and was essentially a very much revised and extended version of the plan he had announced in the EDVAC document. The other three parts were called *Planning and Coding of Problems for an Electronic Computing Instrument* and discussed the efficient use of the machine in the solution of problems. It was in this document that flow charts first came into use, in a form rather different from that seen now. His authorship of the complete report was joint with that of Goldstine, and the first part also with Arthur Burks. Burks had originally worked on the ENIAC project and he left Princeton in 1946 to take up another academic appointment.

In almost all the expository documents written by von Neumann on computing, the reader is drawn to the use of the machine to solve partial differential equations. In one report he illustrates the need for the computer in the numerical solution of these by discussing a particularly difficult non-linear elliptic equation in which about one million multiplications are involved. The fact that a parallel machine performs multiplications, even by repeated additions, much faster than a serial machine, and therefore could solve problems of this type more quickly, was one reason for his choice of this mode of operation.

The other reason was a matter of convenience for the memory. In the IAS computer, delay line memories were not going to be used. Instead, von Neumann hoped to use a memory organ based on the television camera tube or 'iconoscope', the new device to be called a 'selectron'. The research on these was being carried out by RCA (Radio Corporation of America), but their development was a long way behind that of the rest of the computer. Fortunately, the Princeton group learned that F. C. Williams at the University of Manchester was having great success with a rather similar device based on the ordinary television cathode ray tube. Bigelow, the chief engineer, then spent some time in Manchester to learn about these, but by the time he returned to Princeton there was an experimental memory already working satisfactorily.

The Williams tube memory element worked very much like a television picture. Dots were electrically placed on the phosphorous coating of the screen. Each dot represented a '1' in the binary code. The whole area of the screen could not be used as in a television set as the electrostatic charge spread and affected parts of the screen surrounding the original dot. Also the phosphorescence quickly disappeared and had to be renewed cyclically. Even these difficulties were as nothing compared to the alternatives. The IAS computer was built with forty William's tubes, each holding one digit of a forty-digit word, and each tube capable of holding 1024 digits (32 × 32).

Unlike any of the earlier machines, the Princeton computer did not have a synchronised electrical pulse governing the operation of its circuitry. Each circuit was designed to function immediately as it was needed, or ready. This asynchrous circuit design also contributed to the speed of the machine.

When it was finished the computer was relatively small and compact, measuring only about 8 feet long by 2 feet wide by 6 feet high. The memory was built underneath the arithmetic unit. The planned long-term memory was slow to materialise. It was intended that a magnetic tape device should form a secondary memory and that there would be a third one made up from punched tape or cards. The secondary memory proved troublesome; a magnetic wire memory was first used but this was soon removed. Much later it was replaced by a rotating magnetic drum.

The programming was done directly by machine code. Inputs and outputs were first made by punched tape but later IBM punched-card machines were adapted to fill these roles.

This design now seems very antiquated and strange but the resulting computer was a great achievement. The von Neumann machine became a reference point for the design of future computers, and the report already mentioned became a kind of design and operation manual. At Princeton more than a machine was built, the concept of an electronic computer was created. This machine was the arch-patriarch of a dynasty of machines, the great grandfather of the computer industry. Its first progeny were Johnniac (named after the creator of the original machine) made at the Rand Corporation, Maniac (Los Alamos), Avidac, Illiac, Oracle, Ordvac and many others. The machines were never exactly the same as the IAS computer, but they were based on von Neumann's concept. In time, of course, new machines were derived from these near copies, and so a major part of the computerisation of society started. It was not long before IBM brought out machines descended from this line, they were the IBM 701, 704 and so on.

To return to the Princeton machine. It became operational in the spring of 1951, but it was not fully complete until a year later. However, during the summer of 1951 it performed a massive calculation concerned with the development of the hydrogen bomb, in the course of which it ran for 60 days, 24 hours a day. Very few mistakes were discovered when the calculations were checked during the same period. Also relatively few breakdowns occurred. It is significant that it contained only 2,300 thermionic valves. Remember, the ENIAC contained 18,000 and even the EDVAC needed 3,600, together with 1,000 germanium diodes. The IAS computer continued working until 1960, when it was dismantled and sent to the Smithsonian Institution.

Again, it is worth pointing out that computers were important to the military and that their development was in the hands of mathematicians, engineers and scientists. Machines, including the IAS computer, were built to be able to solve problems of great mathematical complexity. They were developed by universities and research centres for mathematics. This is not the case now when most machines are for business use, following the trail blazed by Hollerith in the development of high-speed counting and accounting machines. It is apparent that it was no coincidence that von Neumann worked at Los Alamos as a consultant and as such he had an important hand in the development of the hydrogen bomb, and that the Princeton machine could be used to solve the problems he encountered.

As well as his work on computers, von Neumann was busy with other things. During the early part of the war he wrote a book in conjunction with the economist Oskar Morgenstern on the application of games theory to economics. After the war he became increasingly concerned with consultancies and committee work for the US government. He also worked as a consultant to an oil company and later to IBM. His mathematical research did not stop, although he did not pioneer any new fields of mathematics. The major new venture he explored during the 1950s was the development of automata theory and its connection with biological systems; more about this in the next chapter. At the same time he was recognised and respected as a leader of world mathematics and theoretical physics. He received many honorary degrees and medals and was elected to numerous learned societies and academies throughout the world. From 1951 to 1953 he was President of the American Mathematical Society.

His most important work of this time is regarded as that on atomic energy. As well as his major participation in the development of the thermonuclear bomb, he was one of the leading advisers to the US authorities on the peaceful and military uses of atomic energy. He was a strong advocate of the development of these terrifying weapons. Along with this he had a deep distrust of the Russians and advocated that the USA take a strong, tough line in the Cold War. John von Neumann was now very much an American, he loved the country and found its way of life suited his temperament. In 1955 he was appointed as a US Atomic Energy Commissioner by President Eisenhower. This was, perhaps, the most senior appointment a scientist could hold; it was a great honour, very well paid, and it absorbed all of von Neumann's time. To accept the position he had to leave the Institute of Advanced Study.

Unfortunately, this triumph was not to last for long. After a very painful period, which began with a bone nodule in his shoulder, John von Neumann died of cancer on the 8th February 1957. His contribution to mathematics, computers and science has been recognised worldwide. As a very special posthumous honour a whole volume of the *Bulletin of the American Mathematical Society* has been devoted to his life and work.

CHAPTER TWELVE

Theoretical Developments

SO FAR WE have looked mainly at the development of computing machines. The underlying principles by which they perform their work have been left until this chapter. If one examines the nature of any machine, there is a mechanism which makes it work, this is the electric circuitry of an electronic computer or the metal cogwheels of the Leibniz or Pascal calculators, and one or more principles which underlie the reason the mechanism accomplishes its task. To take a simple example, a bottle opener works because of the principle of the lever.

The electronic computer has a logical structure which the circuits represent in electricity. Since these machines are expected to carry out arithmetic, there has to be some kind of relationship between the logical structure of the machine and the arithmetic operations it performs. Only when these aspects of a computer are settled on can the mechanism by which it operates in terms of electronic systems be developed.

We are normally concerned with decimal, denary or base ten arithmetic which represents numbers in terms of the digits 0, 1, 2, 3, 4, 5, 6, 7, 8, 9. These ten separate characters would each need an electronic character if this was to be the basis of computer arithmetic. This was indeed the case with the ENIAC (18,000 valves) and some early British computers which incorporated a new kind of valve developed for this task. Most computers, however, use a less concise type of arithmetic which has the simplest possible kind of representation, using only the two digits 0 and 1. The use of only two characters to represent information has a long history and occurred even in primitive times, but an arithmetic based only on 0 and 1 was, as far as I know, written down for the first time by Gottfried Leibniz. A note of his made in October 1674 describes binary arithmetic, the binary notation for the first few numbers, and gives examplss of addition and multiplication.

Binary arithmetic uses twos in much the same way as we are accustomed to using tens. (We will talk about binary numbers in terms of our more familiar system to avoid obscurities.) In the decimal system the digits represent units, tens, hundreds, thousands and so on. For example:

1000s	100s	10s	1s
$(1000 = 10^3)$	$(100 = 10^2)$	$(10 = 10^1)$	$(= 10^o)$
1	3	7	5

In the binary system the digits represent units, twos, fours, eights, sixteens, thirty-seconds and so on.

32s	16s	8s	4s	2s	1s
$(32 = 2^5)$	$(16 = 2^4)$	$(8 = 2^3)$	$(4 = 2^2)$	$(2 = 2^1)$	$(1 = 2^o)$
1	0	1	0	1	1

(In the decimal system this is $1 \times 32 + 0 \times 16 + 1 \times 8 + 0 \times 4 + 1 \times 2 + 1 \times 1 = 43$) It can be seen that the decimal system is very compact in comparison to the binary system. 1375 requires only four columns in decimal form, whereas the relatively small number 43 requires six columns in binary form. This disadvantage is very much offset by the advantage of needing only two characters for its representation, and the relative simplicity with which the arithmetic operations of addition, subtraction, multiplication and division can be performed. For example, the addition

$$\begin{array}{r} 101011 \\ {\scriptstyle 1\,1\,1\,1} \\ +\ \underline{100111} \\ {\scriptstyle 1} \\ 1010010 \end{array}$$

is achieved simply by knowing that one and one makes two $(1 + 1 = 2)$ and carrying into the next column.

Multiplication is even easier than addition since anything multiplied by 1 is unchanged and anything multiplied by zero is also zero; the most difficult part is adding together the partial products to reach the answer. For example:

$$
\begin{array}{r}
11011 \quad (27) \\
\times\ 1010 \\
\hline
00000 \\
110110 \\
0000000 \\
{\scriptstyle 1\ 1\ 1} \\
11011000 \\
\hline
100001110 \quad (270)
\end{array}
$$

While binary arithmetic is a lengthy method of working, the speed of computers makes up for this. Most operations are performed in terms of addition; continued addition and column shifting for multiplication, complemented addition for subtraction, and division is performed via subtraction.

The two character arithmetic needs only two states of a device for its representation. Current flowing, or one impulse of current, for '1' and no current for '0'. A switch on for '1' and off for '0'. A component operating for '1' or not operating for '0' is the way these digits are represented by the computer circuits. It so happens that the behaviour of two-state systems is at the same time simple, in that each component is either 'on' or 'off', and capable of performing complex operations, since two-state components can be linked together indefinitely to synthesise arithmetical operations. For instance, many two-state components, initially valves, would be needed to perform the previous examples of binary arithmetic. It was a piece of good fortune that the behaviour of two-state systems in electronic computers could be linked with a logical calculus that had been developed nearly one hundred years earlier by George Boole.

Logic is the study of reason, and for many hundreds of years it was concerned exclusively with Aristotle's limited system. For centuries it had been the dream of philosophers to have a very precise means of representing ideas, and to be able to perform a number of operations on this and draw correct conclusions. This was the preoccupation of Raymond Lull (born 1234) whose system was quite extensive and relied on certain basic ideas in each sphere of knowledge. However, with the increase of knowledge, Lull's logic was left high and dry, because it was unable to progress beyond the limitations and superstitions of his time. The person who was to take hold of this idea was the great mathematician-philosopher Gottfried Leibniz.

Leibniz analysed the notion of a powerful deductive logic for the precise representation of ideas and believed that such a system needed three main parts. First, a precise, unambiguous language with which to specify and write down ideas. It had to apply to all truths. Leibniz realised that it would need to be mainly, or perhaps totally symbolic, since ordinary language is fraught with difficulties when logical exactness is needed. This symbolic language was the *characteristica universalis*. To make deductions on the statements written in this language, a set of logical forms of reasoning was needed. They had to be so powerful and extensive that they would always lead to a conclusion. This was the *calculus ratiocinator*. Leibniz conceived that his goals would be achieved by having a basic set of concepts in terms of which all other things could be defined. It was intended that complicated ideas could be built out of simpler ones, which were themselves built out of even more simple ones, until the basic concepts were reached. There was to be a method of combining these basic concepts in terms of fixed rules in the building of higher notions so that any higher idea could be broken down and analysed in terms of these rules so as to discern its meaning. Thus the rules of combination of primitive ideas governed the meaning of more complex ideas. This part of his logical structure was known as the *ars combinatoria*.

Although Leibniz's idea for a logical analytical calculus was an improvement on all that had gone before, it was doomed to failure. It is extremely doubtful that such an enterprise could ever succeed, and even Leibniz knew that he needed a lot of first-rate thinkers working together to realise it. Apart from a few notes sketching out various ideas, he left no practical elaboration of his scheme. He was so busy that he had little time in which to develop his ideas in detail, but in later years he did seem to regret that he had not done more.

Nearly two hundred years later the first practical logical calculus of this kind was published. This fell far short of Leibniz's good scheme, but, nevertheless, it was to prove of immense importance. In 1849 George Boole published *The Mathematical Analysis of Logic* which was the first statement of Boolean Algebra. Five years later he gave the subject a more elaborate treatment in *An Investigation of the Laws of Thought on which are founded the Mathematical Theories of Logic and Probability*. Boole's goal was to represent the way people think in terms of mathematical statements. Now this idea seems a little naive, because we know that thinking is far more complex than Boole realised. But his logical calculus has succeeded in describing the 'thought' of electronic computers.

George **Boole** was born at Lincoln on the 2nd November 1815. His early interest in scientific pursuits was fostered by his father who, although a cobbler, was interested in optical instruments and made a telescope. At school George received a basic education in reading, writing and arithmetic, but little else. When he left, he went to an establishment offering a commercial education, which might have fitted him for a post as a clerk in some business. This was not enough for him; with the help of a local bookseller and the encouragement of his father he went on to study the languages Latin, Greek, French and Italian, with the intention of entering the Church. He was very successful at this, and not really cut out for the world of commerce. When he was fourteen he made a translation of 'Ode to Spring' by the Greek poet Meleanger which was published in a local newspaper. A schoolmaster accused Boole's father of misrepresentation in allowing his son's work to be published since he, the schoolmaster, did not believe that this could be the work of one so young.

In July 1831, when he was sixteen, George Boole obtained a post as a teacher in a school at Doncaster. This was to be the way he made his living for the next eighteen years, eventually opening his own school. As a schoolmaster he was not a complete success. He was reputed to be an excellent master for very able boys, but he did not have a great deal of patience with those less well-endowed mentally. During his time as a teacher he developed an interest in mathematics, initially because mathematics textbooks were cheap with respect to the amount of knowledge they contained. Boole was later to regret that it took him so long to learn the subject which was to be his claim to fame. However, he eventually mastered it in an original and fresh way which was free from the constraints of a tedious mathematical education where a student was valued mainly for his ability to solve needlessly difficult problems.

Boole published his first work in the newly founded *Cambridge Mathematical Journal* which was edited by his friend Duncan F. Gregory. Gregory was impressed with Boole's ability and recommended that he should submit a paper on one of his important pieces of research to the Royal Society for publication. It was published and it also earned Boole a gold medal for the best piece of work received in the previous three years. This paper contained the D-operator method for solving differential equations, which is familiar to many A'-level students of mathematics.

In 1847 Boole put together his ideas of a logical calculus, a subject which had interested him for some time. The publication of his work was prompted by a dispute between the Scottish philosopher Sir W. Hamilton and the English logician and mathematician Augustus De Morgan. Although his ideas were later extended and elaborated in his *Laws of Thought* . . ., the central parts of his logical calculus were contained in *The Mathematical Analysis of Logic*.

By 1849 his ideas of mathematics and logic were well-known in academic circles and caused him to be held in such high esteem that when Queen's College, Cork was founded, Boole was invited to become its first professor of mathematics. This was a remarkable opportunity, since he had no formal qualifications in the subject.

In Ireland he continued to prosper, being regarded as a very able scholar by his academic friends and colleagues, and a kindly simpleton by the townspeople of Cork. The gentleness and kindness which he and his father had shown to the people of Lincoln was continued in Ireland, even though it was sometimes misinterpreted. Boole married the niece of another professor and they had five daughters, one of whom became a talented mathematician and another of whom was England's first woman professor of chemistry. Boole died on the 8th December 1864 after contracting a severe chill.

Boole's logic was not intended for computer circuitry but as a symbolic model of human thought. His system was made up from sets, x, y, z say; he called them classes. 1 is the universal set, the set of all things under consideration, and 0 is the empty set, the set without any members. Now, for example, the xy is the set of women who wear trousers if x is the set of women and y is the set of things that wear trousers. This can be extended to the set of fat women who wear trousers, xyz, if z is the set of fat things. $x + y$ is the set of things which are x or y, the set of women or things which wear trousers. The distributive law could be used in his system; $x\ (y + z)$, the set of women who wear trousers or are fat is the same as the set of women who wear trousers or the set of fat women. That is $x\ (y + z) = xy + xz$. One important departure from our familiar algebra is that $x^2 = x$ and $x + x = x$. If we write $x . x = x$ it is obvious that the set of women who are women is still the set of women. Similarly, the set of women or the set of women is still the set of women. These rules can be extended, $x^n = x$ and $nx = x$, where n is a whole number greater than 1. From $x^2 = x$ we get $x\ (1 - x) = 0$. Since 1 is the universal set which contains everything under consideration, $1 - x$ is the set of those things which are not women. So $x\ (1 - x)$ is the set of women and the set of things which are not women. Hence $x\ (1 - x) = 0$, the set with no members, the empty set. In fact, $1 - x$ is the complement of x or not x now written as x'. To take subtraction a little further $x - y$ is the set of women who are not trouser wearing things, that is who do not wear trousers; and $y - x$ is the set of trouser wearing things that are not women. Clearly $x + y = y + x$, and addition is commutative as is multiplication $xy = yx$, but $x - y \neq y - x$.

Later in the nineteenth century, Boole's logic was improved by W. S. Jevons, E. Schroder and the American logician C. S. Pierce. Schroder and Pierce discovered the peculiar distribution law of addition and multiplication, that is $x + y.z = (x + y)(x + z)$. During the first part of the present century there was a tendency for logicians to experiment with difficult sets of rules, or axioms, which generated a given mathematical structure. Among the many who did this with Boole's system were E. V. Huntington and and H. M. Sheffer. The usual modern way of stating the rules for Boolean algebra is an elaboration of one of a number of systems due to Huntington. A summary of these is:

    commutative laws $x + y = y + x$, $x.y = y.x$
    associative laws $x + y + z = (x + y) + z$, $x.y.z = (x.y)z$
    distributive laws $x.(y + z) = x.y + x.z$, $x + (y.z) = (x + y)(x + z)$

sum rules $x + x' = 1$ (where x' is the complement of, or not x)
$\qquad x + 1 = 1, x + 0 = x, x + x = x$
product rules $x.x' = 0, x.0 = 0, x.1 = x, x^2 = x.x = x$
absorption rules $x + x.y = x, x + x'.y = x + y$
De Morgan laws $(x + y)' = x'.y', (x.y)' = x' + y'$.

Boolean algebra is used in many branches of mathematics and logic, and sometimes the signs $\cap$ or $\wedge$ replace . and $\cup$ or $\vee$ replace $+$.

The use of Boolean algebra to represent electrical switching circuits was probably first noticed by the physicist P. Ehrenfest in 1910. It was not, however, until the 1930s when such an application was seen to be of importance, because of the cost of labour and materials for the building of large electrical circuits. Claude E. Shannon, a research student of Vannevar Bush at MIT, realised the power of Boolean algebra for simplifying relay and switching circuits and developed the idea to the stage where it could be of practical use. It is quite possible that he had never heard of Ehrenfest's idea when he published his Boolean algebra theory of switching circuits in 1938.

As an example of the application of Boolean algebra to the design of circuits, consider the one illustrated, where a,b,c are switches in the closed position (current flowing) and a' is switch a in the open position (no current). Is this circuit the simplest (and cheapest) one which will accomplish the task?

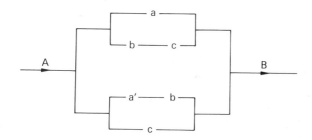

The current is required to flow from A to B. Let C represent the current, then in Boolean terms

$C \equiv [a + bc] + [a'b + c]$
$\quad \equiv a + bc + a'b + c$
$\quad \equiv a + a'b + c + cb$.

Now $a + a'b$ is $a + b$ by one of the absorption rules and

c + c b is c by the other absorption rule.

∴ C ≡ a + b + c

So the simplest equivalent circuit is:

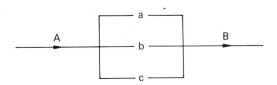

Shannon was destined to play a considerable part in the theory of circuits and computation. But perhaps his greatest achievement is his synthesis of the mathematical theory of communication. He popularised the term 'bit', meaning binary digit. Although its derivation is sometimes attributed to him, in his *The Mathematical Theory of Communication* he credited J. W. Tukey with first suggesting it.

The development of computers was an embryonic science in the 1940s and the seminal ideas were likely to come from all areas of knowledge. One of the important notions for the logical design of computers, which John von Neumann quickly latched on to, came from two scientists, Warren S. McCulloch and Walter Pitts. In their work on a mathematical model of the way nerves work which was published in 1943, they developed a kind of ideal nerve and a logical calculus of nervous activity. This was based on their simple, idealised model of a nerve cell or neuron, which did not pretend to be a biological description. The McCulloch and Pitts cells were devices which could be activated by certain numbers of impulses, they would then pass on one impulse to another neuron. Certain nerves could be inhibited by impulses. With various combinations of activation and inhibition inputs, a wide variety of neurons could be devised.

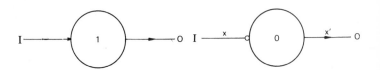

A neuron which fires at O (output) when one impulse is received at I (input). Its function is to delay for one pulse.
A neuron which is firing repeatedly unless a pulse is received at I. Its function is to express 'not' in which case it is inhibited.

A truth table for 'not' expressed in Boolean algebra with '1' indicating 'current' and '0' 'no current'.

x	x′ (not x)
0	1
1	0

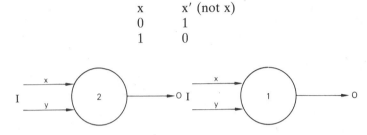

A neuron to represent 'and'. A neuron to represent 'or'.

x	y	x.y (x and y)		x	y	x + y (x or y)
0	0	0		0	0	0
1	0	0		1	0	1
0	1	0		0	1	1
1	1	1		1	1	1

Von Neumann used these cells in his designs for the logical operations of computers. In these, from numerous types of neurons, the logical structures for the various kinds of arithmetic unit can be fabricated. More exotic neurons can accomplish combinations of these operations much more economically. Indeed, one of the most important types used by von Neumann is that which performs the Sheffer stroke operation. Originally this was written by H. M. Sheffer as $x|y$, (hence the name); according to the system above for Boolean algebra it is written $(x.y)'$

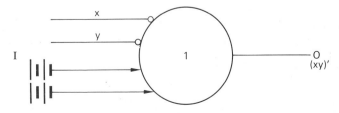

|ı|ı, the usual sign for a battery, indicates that the input is continually receiving pulses. Von Neumann showed that by connecting these devices in certain ways the three logical operations 'not', 'or' and 'and' could be replaced and so any logic circuit could be built up entirely from Sheffer strokes. This unit has become so common in modern computer design that it is now called the NAND function, indicating 'and and not'.

x	y	x|y $\equiv (x.y)'$ $\equiv$ NAND
0	0	1
1	0	1
0	1	1
1	1	0

Components which perform another operation NOR can also be connected together in various ways to synthesise any logic circuit.

NOR neuron

x	y	$(x + y)'$ $\equiv$ NOR
0	0	1
1	0	0
0	1	0
1	1	0

These cells are still frequently used to illustrate the functions of various logical components in computers, but often in a simpler and more stylised way than that proposed by von Neumann. Before we leave this topic, it is important to point out the conclusion of McCulloch and Pitts' paper, which contains more than the invention of a useful notation. Their main result was that any set of operations which can be specified completely and unambiguously in a finite (that is, not unlimited) set of words can be performed by a network of these neurons.

As an aside from the main business of this chapter, it is worth remarking that von Neumann and Goldstine invented the flow chart. The flow chart is known by all those who prepare programs for computers. It is now made up correctly in a clear and straightforward way from a well-known and fairly standard set of symbols. The inventors intended a plan of what they were going to perform on a computer. But what with the mathematics, the code in which the instructions are described and the almost complete use of rectangles whatever the type of decision or instruction, the appearance is very different from modern flow charts. The fact that the planning of computer tasks now looks very different is a consequence of many things: the increase in the size of memories and the advent of high level languages, as well as the standardisation of flow chart symbols.

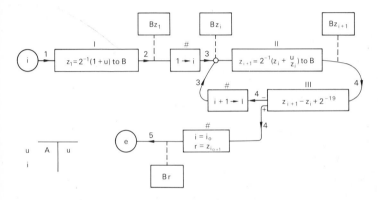

This diagram represents a program involving numerical analysis, in which $v = \sqrt{u}$ is computed. It is taken from their *Planning and Coding of Problems for an Electronic Computing Instrument* (Part II, volume I) which was published in 1947.

In following the track of Boolean algebra and von Neumann's work we have gone ahead in time of what is probably the most important theoretical result in the field of computation. Alan Turing's famous work of 1936, *On Computable Numbers, with an application to Entscheidungsproblem*, showed how much could be achieved with simple computational procedures. His computer was a primitive theoretical machine; nobody would waste their time building a practical model. The Turing machine, as it is now known, is made up from a tape which is divided into squares; a device which can read, write and erase marks on a square of the tape; a mechanism which can move the tape either one square to the right or one to the left (or not move it at all), and a table of rules which tells it how to behave. This behaviour consists of changing between several specified states and performing the correct action in response to what it 'reads' on each square of the tape.

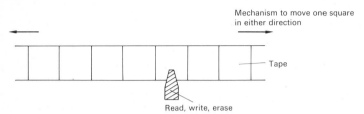

To learn how the Turing machine works, look at the first line of the table of instructions: X, p|X, q, + 1. This shows that if the machine is in state X and it 'sees' p written on the tape, then it must erase p and write q on the same square, move one square to the right but stay in state X. For example, before the machine starts to operate, let the tape be:

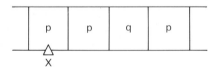

After one move it becomes

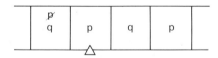

The same operation is performed again because the machine is in the same state and it encounters an identical symbol on the tape.

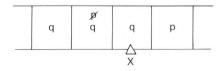

Now we require different instructions from the table; the complete table of instructions is

Environment		Operation		
State	Symbol	State	Symbol	Move
X	p	X	q	+1
X	q	Y	p	+1
Y	p	Y	q	−1 (left)
Y	q	X	q	0 (halt)

Hence, the next move will be to replace the *q* with a *p*, move one square to the right and go into state *Y*.

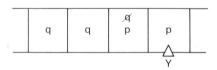

Next *p*, is replaced by *q* the move is one place to the left, and the state remains as *Y*.

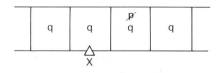

The same operation is repeated again.

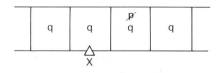

Finally, the machine in state *Y* 'reads' *q* which tells it to 'write' *q*, change into state *X* and halt.

This simple instruction table illustrates the behaviour of the Turing machine; it also gives some indication of how lengthy, tedious and moronic this process is. To carry out even the simplest pieces of arithmetic, instruction tables with many lines are required and the number of steps needed for the calculation is even longer. For instance, to subtract two p's from three p's requires a table of ten operations and fifteen steps.

Clearly, the importance of the Turing machine lies neither in its conciseness of definition nor in its speed in performing its task. However, if a table can be constructed to give the machine a description of how to behave at each moment, then the instructions given can be executed by a Turing machine. Turing did not stop at the machine which was governed by one table, he showed that there was a general or universal Turing machine which could carry out the task of any special Turing machine.

The universal Turing machine is only slightly different in design from the special one. It has a tape which can be extended indefinitely. On this tape is the initial set of rules for the special machine to operate on, together with its table of instructions, a description of its initial state and a means of identifying that this is a particular special Turing machine. On to the individual tape can be placed these very complete descriptions of any, and, at least in theory, every special Turing machine. In operation, the universal machine is excruciatingly slow, having repeatedly to move backwards and forwards between the part of the tape where it receives its instructions and the part where it performs its operations, each time marking its place. The table of operations to allow a universal machine to simulate the work in any special machine, is very large.

The fact that a universal machine exists in theory which can carry out the work of any machine which can be described precisely in terms of a table of instructions suggested that a general purpose, or perhaps, a universal purpose, computer would work in theory; it only remained for it to be built. We have seen how this work was taken up in a practical way by the British government and Alan Turing during the war, and how it influenced von Neumann. Whether or not the other pioneers of the time were aware of this is not known. In one sense it might be said that Turing proved the obvious; after all, had not Babbage outlined a general purpose machine in his design for the analytical engine. While Turing's result was not really needed by those who already had the inclination to make a practical computer, it gave them and many others the support that their projects were theoretically feasible. It occurs far more often than is usually realised that scientists chase goals that are not theoretically attainable and so can never be realised in practice. There is a story in which a group of chemists tried to synthesise a compound which had molecules containing an atom of arsenic. After nine months of work a junior member of the team, while playing about with a set of model atoms, found that no matter how he tried he could not squeeze the one which represented arsenic into the remaining part of the molecule. Simply, the sizes of the actual atoms were incompatible and the arsenic compound could not be made. But six chemists had worked nine months with reagents, glassware, and heaters!

Von Neumann was fascinated with Turing's ideas. He spent much time attempting to examine their consequences and extend their application. Turing's machines and the like have frequently been called automatons and the field of study has become known as automata theory. Von Neumann eventually devised a self-reproducing automaton. He showed that it was theoretically possible for a machine to construct a replica of itself given a finite set of instructions and access to the parts it required. This is perhaps not as surprising as it might at first seem, because the biologists have discovered the mechanism of replication of RNA and DNA molecules. Unfortunately, von Neumann began to make progress in the theory of self-reproducing automata at a time when he was very busy with other things. His ill-health and death prevented him from continuing this work.

The notion that a machine can reproduce itself seems to have an element of science fiction. Indeed, the very idea is frightening to some people, including scientists. That it is theoretically possible to have such machines suggests to them that one day they will become a practical reality. Fortunately, perhaps, the gap between the theory and its realisation is still very large.

At the beginning of the second half of the twentieth century there was a certain distrust of new machines. This included computers, but it also included many things that had come out of the war, and others that might still be unknown because of the secrecy surrounding them. Remember, the world was still trembling with fear and anger at the advent of nuclear weapons! Computers were often thought of, or even possibly described, as 'electronic brains'. Electronic brains and robots were common in the science fiction of the time. The featuring of robots possibly increased because of the war-time work on servomechanics and the improvement of control systems. Indeed, now there must be very few space films or television programmes which do not include a very 'intelligent' computer. Often, everything but the plot is carried out by this 'intelligence'. At the time under consideration there was a dual feeling towards electronic computers. They were fine if they helped us and kept their place, but they were derided if they were of superior 'intelligence' to us. Those who were concerned directly, or indirectly, as were people as far apart as the press and philosophers, were divided into two camps; those who welcomed the computer and those who accepted its contribution to our science and culture with anxiety. In the end, the view prevailed that was probably first described by the Countess of Lovelace, Babbage's friend and helper who indicated that machines were only able to carry out the instructions of their programmers. The view gradually developed that computers were inanimate imbeciles which had to be told every step with extreme care and precision.

However, this was not the end of the speculation. If computers could play chess, solve mathematical problems and decide who had written a certain piece of literature, were they not exhibiting intelligence? As cleverer machines were built, this 'intelligence' seemed to be more than that of an imbecile. The question of the 'intelligence' of the 'electronic brain' eventually begged the answer in terms of the speed of performing operations and the very size of the computer. Those who had, or would explore the answer to 'How clever is a computer?' found that they became stuck with human intelligence before they even tackled that of the machine. Psychologists had no clear cut answer to the question of 'What is intelligence?' They had several models and lots of tests, but no answer that could be used to analyse the nature of machine intelligence. If the question was framed in terms of 'thought' or 'consciousness', the psychologists and philosophers could offer lots of ideas and theories, but the human organism was so complex that no definite, full answers could be given. Men and computers were incomparable. An 'electronic brain' was no longer a magnified replica of the human brain, it was something very different. The intelligence of machines developed as a definite subject in its own right, and psychologists continued to discover and speculate about the nature of the intelligence of animate objects. Obviously, there have been collaborations between the two fields of knowledge, but not to the extent that might at one time have been expected. It is certainly very obvious that machines can exhibit some very 'intelligent' behaviour.

The 'intelligence' of computers was examined in 1950 by Alan Turing in 'Computing Machines and Intelligence' which was published in *Mind*, a leading British journal of philosophy. He examined many objections to computers possessing intelligence and refuted them all easily. However, he offered no real theory of computer 'thought', only his belief that computers were 'intelligent'. In his discussion, he had pointed out that the view of Lady Lovelace and many more modern theorists was suspect because even then they frequently did not really know what to expect from the output of a reliable computer, like the one at Manchester which he had programmed himself. Of course, like the psychologists, he realised the difficulties with the question: 'What is intelligence?' So he devised a test.

There is a game that is sometimes played at parties in which messages are passed between three people. The people are a man and woman, who are in separate rooms, and a player who does not know which room contains the woman and which the man. The object of the game is for the player to determine which room the woman is in by passing only written messages. Obviously questions like 'Are you a woman?' are valueless because the hiding players will lie. It is necessary for the guessing player to decide on the subtleties of the answers which might indicate aspects of masculinity or femininity. Clearly, emotions and personalities are involved as well as intelligence. Turing's intention was to substitute one of the hiders for a computer. The object of the game is then to decide which room the human is in. (Communication would, by the nature of things, need to be via a teleprinter.) Personality and emotions, I think, would cloud the decision, whatever the outcome, leaving the nature of 'intelligence' still rather obscure. But do computers have personalities? Are they always cold or can they be friendly? Can they show love or anger? Do these aspects just have meanings for humans? But what if a computer is sufficiently intelligent to mimic friendship and love (or any other of these personality attributes) during Turing's test?

At about the same time as Turing was writing this paper, W. Grey Walter, a physiologist working in England, constructed a number of mechanical 'organisms'. One of these, called *Machina speculatrix*, was made to simulate the work of two nerve cells and was composed of two valves, two relays, two capacitors, two motors and two batteries. One of the 'nerves' operated by sensitivity to light, for which there was a photoelectric cell, and the second was a touch receptor, for which an electrical contact was used. With this small number of simple components, *Machina speculatrix* exhibited a startlingly complex and unpredictable behaviour pattern. This must give some indication as to the depths and complexity of computer 'intelligence'!

CHAPTER THIRTEEN

From the Pioneers to the Modern Computer

IN THE EARLY 1950s there were many individual machines. These had been built by universities, government agencies and a few companies. Almost all of these computers had the trademarks of the pioneers: dedicated designers and engineers, a design goal which could be either specific or perhaps somewhat vague but always the technological means of achieving it required scientific and engineering development as it progressed, and financial support from government agencies or from funds allocated to research, from which any financial return was expected to be in the long term. Most, if not all, of these early machines were intended to work on lengthy and complex calculations, such as were required by science and engineering, even though a large element of repetition may be involved. In effect, the computer was still seen as an electronic brain, replacing that of the scientist and performing his complicated work in a much shorter time than he could.

As we have seen, there was already a considerable involvement of automatic machines in the handling of the vast amounts of relatively simple data which were involved with census taking and accountancy. In fact, many large organisations already used punched card systems and electrical accounting machines. These systems were a very profitable part of such firms as British Tabulating Machine Co (BTM) International Business Machines (IBM) and the National Cash Register Corporation (NCR). The executives of these firms, and many others, were aware of the potential importance of electronic computers to their businesses. While vast amounts of capital were required to enter the business of making computers, many courageous and forsighted companies committed themselves to developing electronic machines for processing vast amounts of data in a fairly simple way, as well as for solving more complex problems. Once businesses became involved with the view to making money, rather than just fulfilling government contracts, the time of the pioneers was over and the age of the electronic computer had begun. The change in emphasis from the pioneer to the firm was highly desirable, but it took place gradually. There will always be the special purpose, one-off computer project designed by researchers outside the economic constraints of industry, but even they have usually been pleased to have the hardware built by industrial contractors.

As we have seen, the Manchester University Computer was successfully manufactured and sold in small quantities by Ferranti Ltd., and the Pilot Ace was developed into the English Electric Deuce. The result of an interchange of ideas between M. V. Wilkes, D. R. Hartree and H. H. Goldstine and the J. Lyons Catering Company as early as 1947 resulted in financial support for the Cambridge EDSAC and the eventual development of the commercial LEO (Lyons Electronic Office) computers. UNIVAC 1, from the Mauchly and Eckert stable, came into operation in the USA in 1951 and was the first computer designed for commercial applications. The following year the IBM 650 model was introduced for a similar purpose. After a long gestation period the first native English commercial computer, LEO 1, was completed in 1953.

These early manufactured machines were, by modern standards, large, clumsy, delicate and expensive for their performance. They required a large air-conditioned room, had a huge appetite for electricity and were subject to valve failures. There was a large variety of memory types available. The Williams' tubes, delay lines and numerous other kinds of magnetic and electrostatic devices were still used. None of the storage methods designed up to that time had sufficient advantages to be a clear winner. This part of computer design was, however, soon to be settled in a new and very favourable way.

In 1947 Andrew D. Booth, who was a pioneer of small computers at the University of London, and Jay W. Forrester, independently suggested the coincident current magnetic core memory. Although Booth lectured on this subject in London, it was Forrester who became involved with the development of the idea. Forrester worked, like Vannevar Bush, at MIT where he had founded the Servomechanism Laboratory. From 1944 onwards he was involved with Project Whirlwind which began as a projected analogue computer for the analysis of stability and control of aircraft but was eventually completed in 1951 as a large digital computer for the US Navy. Ferrite core storage was also independently pioneered by Jan A. Rajchman at the Radio Corporation of America (RCA). The iron rings, which make up these stores, are now tiny (less than the size of a pin head); while Rajchman was developing these, he made them the size of an aspirin tablet with a pill press, like those once used by pharmacists. In 1953 IBM became involved with a defence computer for the early warning system which was being built at the Lincoln Laboratory of MIT. This involvement was instrumental in the commercial use of core memories. They were first used in the IBM 704 and 705 machines which became available in 1955 and they replaced the original memory intended for the 704 computer.

The early warning computer, SAGE, was one of the largest ever built. It weighed 113 tons and contained 58,000 valves. It processed the data available from the radar of the military network in real-time, that is it processed the data and reported on the situation immediately.

The 700 series of computers marked the beginning of commercial involvement with large computers at IBM. These were powerful machines right from their inception with the 701. There were large commercial successes with the 704, essentially a scientific machine, and the commercial data processing 705.

By the late 1950s a large variety of computers was available for purchase. Of course, they could not be bought and delivered the same week. Orders were placed, the computer was built, often with modifications to suit the buyer, and months later it was delivered. A model rated as successful might have sold only a few machines, especially in Britain. In the USA commercial success was a little more dramatic: the IBM 650 model sold about 1,000 and the original estimate of the cost of the 704 was based on a market of 50 machines.

Computers were still very much the province of the university, the research organisation and the very large firm. Only in the early 1960s was it possible to expect every university, polytechnic or large organisation to use its own computer. Smaller companies often bought computer time; and still do! Most machines were still used for scientific purposes in England, but the balance was soon to change, with data processing applications becoming the most important in terms of the number of machines, and their value as profits to the computer manufacturing industry. What brought about this change in use had a lot to do with the biggest change the electronic computer had to go through.

The inevitable metamorphosis started several years before its effects were incorporated into computers with the invention of the transistor in 1947 by William B. Shockley, John Bardeen and Walter H. Brattain. These scientists, who worked at the Bell Telephone Laboratories, were awarded the Nobel Prize for their invention in 1956. Ever since the invention of the diode by Sir Ambrose Fleming in 1904, thermionic valves had been the important component in the rapidly developing field of electronics. Only a few years after this event, W. H. Eccles and F. W. Jordan made the development of electronic computers possible by devising a circuit with a pair of valves which had two stable states. This invention in 1919 allowed information to be stored electronically. However, the success which the early computer pioneers had in overcoming problems of valve reliability and the development of relatively reliable valve circuits in commercial computers, did not mean the problem had vanished. Valves also occupied a lot of space, were fairly expensive and used a lot of electricity. A device which could perform the same function, at least as far as a digital computer was concerned, and be smaller, cheaper and more reliable, was bound to have devastating effects.

It is, perhaps, surprising that transistors were not incorporated in computers much earlier. But at first, transistors were rather expensive, mainly because factories were not able to manufacture them in bulk. It took some time to realise their potential applications, as well as their limitations, and to develop suitable circuitry. So although their importance to computers was realised soon after their invention, the first computer to use transistors was the small research machine at the University of Manchester, in 1953. The first commercially available transistor computers came in 1958, and included the British Elliott 802.

In 1959 IBM introduced the first of their highly successful 1400 series of transistorised computers. The 1401 sold more than 10,000 models and brought the electronic computer within the range of medium-sized businesses in America. One of the most powerful computers of this time was STRETCH, built by IBM for the US Atomic Energy Commission, at the Los Alamos Scientific Laboratory. It contained 150,000 transistors and represented the most sophisticated computing facility of the time; it continued the tradition begun with the ENIAC in dealing with the mathematics involved in the design of atomic weapons.

Since the beginning of serious commercial involvement in the manufacture of computers, there has been an important field of development concerned with the so called computer peripherals; the remote access memories, input/output equipment and associated apparatus. Speeds increased for gaining access to memory stores and for the transfer of information. Card readers and printers, which were extremely important to the efficiency of a computing facility because of the speed of processing and the capacity of work it could handle, went through many evolutionary phases.

At the beginning of the 1950s the computer programmers were the scientists, mathematicians and engineers who had developed and built the machines. They had a familiarity with the working of the electronic circuits, the way the circuits represented data and operations, and they also had such other knowledge of their specific machines that made programming perhaps not easy, but certainly a skill which they could understand and master. Organisations buying computers for the first time had the difficulty of finding people to operate them. The pioneers had largely worked with machine code, which gave precise instructions for every operation the machine made. This required a great deal of knowledge and skill; and so to train new programmers, first able people had to be found and then much time had to be expended on their training. There was always a problem in finding the talented and trained people to operate a new computer.

Moves towards solving the difficulties inherent in computer

programming went on from the beginning, but it was not until the high-level languages were introduced that this task became relatively easy. IBM introduced FORTRAN (FORmula TRANslation) for use on their 704 model in 1957, but it had already been under development for three years. ALGOL (ALGOrhythmic Language), which had been developed by an international committee and had originally been named IAL (Internal Algebraic Language) became available the following year. COBOL (COmmon Business Oriented Language) was initiated by the US Department of Defense, and was first used in December 1959. Unlike the two earlier languages which were science orientated, it was intended for computer use in business and commerce.

By the end of the 1950s the development of the computer had advanced from the one-off valve machine for government or scientific purposes, which took a great deal of time and expertise to program, to large, fast, easily-programmed machines, which were as common in data processing applications as they were in defence and scientific uses. At the beginning of the 1960s there were over forty different types of computer available in Britain, from the early production valve machines, to the latest transistor models. Throughout the non-communist countries there were now over 10,000 computers in existence, most of which were in the USA. The few computers that Russia possessed were made in Britain because IBM refused to supply them on the specific instructions of their chairman Thomas J. Watson Jnr.

Development of the computer was now inextricably linked to developments in electronics. Transistors had largely replaced thermionic valves in situations where power amplification was not required, but there was room for greater improvement. Although electronic gadgetry had been common in homes and industry for many years, probably the greatest users and developers are connected with government agencies. Once the transistor was in common use, the US Defense Department and the developing space industry through NASA stimulated the development of miniature components because of the space limitations in missiles and satellites. The US National Bureau of Standards initiated 'Project Tinteroy', with the object of supporting the development of electronic components in a standard rectangular shape which could be close packed, rather than the traditional cylindrical form of valves, resistors and capacitors. There was also a confidence among engineers, that now that a simple and small substitute for the valve had been found, then similar progress could be made with the more simple resistors and capacitors. Indeed, the early 1960s was a period of rapid development in solid state technology, and the integrated circuit, in which a slice of silicon was treated and fashioned in such a way that it contained all the transistors, capacitors, resistors and interconnections necessary to perform some useful purpose was produced. By 1964 these were available for use in computers. They replaced many of the traditional electronic components, with a subsequent saving of space, power consumption and cost.

By the mid-1960s a combination of the price and availability of computers, familiarity with high-level programming languages and the increasing availability of trained personnel all combined to cause the computer to be seen as a desirable piece of equipment by many organisations. Whether the increase in the amount of data at the time was a cause of the increase in the number of computers, or the effect of the early computerised society, is of little consequence, it spurred many organisations to invest a large amount of money in the new data processing technology. Companies of various sizes required machines which were suitable for their needs. They wanted a system of machines which had the right speed, storage and processing capacities and which could be added to as their businesses increased. With the incorporation of integrated circuits into a new generation of hardware, many computer manufacturers took the opportunity to introduce a series of compatible computers and peripheral devices capable of fulfilling the needs of a wide spectrum of companies and organisations. In 1964 IBM launched its System 360 which embodied these concepts. A year or so later the amalgamated English Electric Leo Marconi Computers Ltd. initiated their System 4 machines.

Integrated circuits and associated technology reduced the size of computers. A machine with the same power as a large room full of valve or even transistor circuits could be housed in the corner of an office. The development of remote access memory facilities also reduced the amount of space needed.

Very often the large cabinets of tapes were replaced by a few magnetic discs, all in the same unit. For those users who wanted only a small machine, a new computer style was developed. In 1965 the Digital Equipment Corporation brought out the first general purpose mini-computers, the PDP-8 and PDP-5, the latter costing about £9,000. These were followed by machines from Honeywell, Hewlett-Packard and Xerox Data Systems. There had, however, already been a few special mini-computers developed for aerospace applications by Burroughs, Hughes and Univac. Mini-computers were often machines where, at least, the input and output devices could be placed on the top of a desk, with little more space needed for the rest of the equipment.

It is difficult to make superlative generalisations about the growth of the use of computers, but if ever there was a time when the computer took off it was in the 1960s. From the 10,000 computers in 1960, there were 30,000 by 1965 and 100,000 by 1970, a ten-fold increase. In 1970 there were over 60,000 of these machines in use in the USA, with about 6,000 in Britain.

Also by 1970 the number of large mainframe computer manufacturers had declined through amalgamation in Britain. IBM increasingly dominated the world trade in large computers and in that year they launched a new series of machines, the System 370. This system possessed all the advances gained by the computer industry from the developments in integrated circuits. Circuits became so tiny that microscopes were needed to see the components. It is almost meaningless to talk about size in the age of microelectronics, since the sizes of components and circuits decreases almost daily. The System 370 possessed a solid state memory in place of the older ferrite core type, and important developments produced a new way of saving space in the central immediate access memory by what was called 'virtual memory', in which information was continually transferred between the immediate and remote access sites, so as to maximise the overall performance of the computer.

By 1970 computing was the occupation of many people. The problem of the shortage of trained labour had been solved initially by a combination of means; now people to fill the vast range of computer personnel functions were being trained in the technical colleges and universities. Now also, an engineer or scientist expected to have access to a computer and was skilled in presenting his problem and handling the machine. Needless to say, companies with a large amount of paperwork expected it to be done on an electronic data handling system, the central part of which was a digital computer. The training of personnel demanded the need for a simple, high-level programming language and the need was met in 1965 when BASIC (Beginners All Purpose Symbolic Instruction Code) was developed at Dartmouth College in the United States by J. Kemeny and T. Kurtz. BASIC has proved so popular that it has displaced the more complex and powerful high-level languages in their simpler and less specialised applications.

During the 1970s the trend in computer design was towards small machines, but there were a few notable achievements in the other direction. ILLIAC IV at the University of Illinois was one of the largest machines of the time, being made up of 64 independent processing units that can operate simulatenously or individually. It was built by the Burroughs Corporation and came into operation around 1972. Very large machines continued to be made for research, scientific and military purposes. The phenomenal Cray computers, made by Cray Research Inc., were sometimes designated supercomputers; and, although its physical dimensions were not large, the Cray – 1 had a memory capacity of well over one million 64-bit words. It had an estimated purchase price of $8,000,000. As the computer evolved, increasing complexity usually indicated greater flexibility and the emphasis in large computers was on the capacity and versatility of a whole system, with a huge variety of input and output devices, including remote terminals and various types of memory devices. Frequently more than one computer was incorporated in a data processing network. In July 1981 it was said that the largest system was that at McDonnell Douglas Automation in St. Louis, where a 450 foot long room houses eight large IBM machines and a number of other smaller machines. However, it is dangerous to quote superlatives in the field of computing, probably by the time the reader sees these words, the record(s) will be held somewhere else.

The rapid development of computing in terms of the proliferation of hardware (the machines) and software (the programs) has not always had a beneficial effect. Since the first high-level languages began to emerge during the middle 1950s, many hundreds if not thousands of types, versions and varieties of languages have come into use. A point has been reached where one installation may use many of these, and an organisation may have many computing laboratories, which further increases the variety of languages in use. In an attempt to combat this, the United States Defense Department at the Pentagon, Washington, initiated the development of a new language to replace the numerous ones already in use in its various departments and installations. One language for all purposes, whether business, scientific, logistic or instructional is a very tall order, but the saving of money was estimated at many hundreds of millions of dollars. The development project was initiated in 1975, and the new language ADA, named after Ada Lovelace, the helper and protege of Charles Babbage, is just beginning to be received and evaluated by the computing world. Whether ADA will fulfil the purpose it has been intended for, and replace a whole group of languages, remains to be seen.

It is not the purpose of this book to describe the developments in software and computer applications. Suffice it to say that these have paralleled the development of the hardware, and that one of the most important achievements has been the creation of high resolution graphics facilities of a standard suitable for the detailed design of many things, including buildings and machines.

The large mainframe computers costing a vast amount of money are still developed and sold in high demand, but the advent of large-scale integration of electronic components with the development of silicon chip technology has led to smaller, cheaper machines with relatively large computing capacity. Mainframe computers are physically small compared with the monsters of two decades ago, minis are smaller and of considerable use to many scientific, engineering and commercial enterprises. Their cost is a few thousand pounds compared with a few hundred thousand for a mainframe, but their capacity is that of a mainframe of a few years ago. In only ten years the cost of a computer per bit of memory has declined fifty-fold. Thus for a few thousand pounds capital outlay, a modest sum in present times (but magnificent by the standards of twenty years ago) a powerful computer can be at the disposal of a small commercial or scientific enterprise.

A little lower down the scale in terms of price and complexity come the so-called microcomputers, whose facilities are more limited than those of the larger minis, but as time has passed the distinction between the two kinds has blurred a little. Originally, the micros were simply smaller and cheaper computers than the available minis, but they have emerged as a fairly distinct group which, within limits imposed by the type of peripheral equipment such as disc drive memories, printers and graphics packages, can be versatile and relatively powerful. Perhaps the best way to characterise a microcomputer is that it is small and cheap, costing only a few hundred pounds. As time has passed the distinction between micros, minis and mainframe computers has merged into a continuum, so that, whereas there are obvious examples of the three size and cost types, some micros are nearly as versatile as minis, and many minis are nearly as powerful as mainframe machines.

With the advent of the microcomputer almost every secondary school and probably all colleges have Apples, Commodore Pets or Research Machines 380Z computers. Also few scientific, engineering or business enterprises are without computing facilities of some type or size, if they have a definite use for them. Even the private individual with less than £100 can have his own small microcomputer. However, not always, and perhaps not even often do the purposes to which these miniature machines are put resemble those which the pioneers had in mind as being of use and benefit to society.

It is now necessary for us to return to the theme of the development of automatic calculation, which we left with the developments of Charles Babbage. Up to the time of Babbage the new inventions were calculators rather than computers and the development of calculators continued to have a parallel, but slow evolution along with computers. Mechanical devices for basic arithmetic calculations, and sometimes with facilities appropriate to accounting or more novel scientific or engineering applications, were to be found in many offices and laboratories. These machines performed a spectrum of useful tasks, but their size and the limitations inherent in the machines restricted them to simple and relatively small calculations performed slowly. In the applications where they were most useful, their capabilities were sufficient. The only desire for improvement came in making these machines cheaper, easier to use, and very much less noisy. They were just too large and too expensive to prevent them from being adopted as personal articles. More than one famous scientist has had to wait in a queue to use the one calculator in a university laboratory.

With the advent of solid state integrated circuits, the calculator was reduced to a pocket size, silent machine, which soon became cheap enough to be bought by anyone who had the need or desire for one. The technology used was essentially that of the computer, but on a much smaller scale. The use of the calculator, however, is very different from that of the computer. The calculator is essentially an electronic means of performing something which can be done by the schoolchild, housewife or scientist on a piece of paper, possibly with the use of tables. It reduces mental exertion and prevents the tedium inherent in arithmetic calculation, whereas the computer processes vast amounts of simple or complex information quickly. For the calculator speed and repetition are not the important features; for a modern computer they are the essence of its usefulness. The functions of the calculator are not very different from the logarithms of Napier. Hopefully these little electronic machines will soon replace all those tables. Neither logarithms nor calculators can do what is done in every minute fraction of a second by a computer, even though the complexity of the actual arithmetic involved may be similar. However, a calculator may possibly have the facility to do calculations at least as complicated as some done by many computers.

Frequently the calculator may be of more use to the scientist than the computer. A computer has to be programmed which is a time-consuming process. If only one calculation is to be performed this may well be performed more quickly by pressing the buttons and waiting for the answer on a calculator. The facilities on calculators have increased to include the means of obtaining the values of many functions which were once usually available from tables. Logarithmic, trigonometric and statistical functions are often included on these devices, together with a number of subroutines for common types of arithmetic and statistical calculations. In fact, with the more sophisticated machines, they can save much of the labour which would otherwise be required to perform a lengthy paper and pencil task, or to write a computer program.

The distinction between calculators and computers is now less obvious than it was; some of the more expensive and involved machines have programs, printers and memories. No doubt these fill a need of some kind, but the basic type of calculator performing $+$, $-$, x, $\div$ and percentage calculations is even more important now than it was in the times of Pascal and Leibniz.

The calculator and computer almost certainly have not reached the end of their evolution, even though they now affect so many facets of life. To emerge in the future worthy of being called a pioneer in the complex and intense field of computing, a person will have to do such a huge amount in terms of new contributions to knowledge that they will indeed be a remarkable man or woman.

Further Reading

The reader interested in following the history of computers in more detail may like to consult the following books.

General History of Computing
Three excellent and complementary books are:
GOLDSTINE, HERMAN H., *The Computer from Pascal to von Neumann, Princeton University Press, Princeton, 1972.*
METROPOLIS, N., HOWLETT, J. and ROTA, GIAN-CARLO, *A History of Computing in the Twentieth Century*, Academic Press, New York, 1980.
RANDELL, BRIAN (editor) *The Origins of Digital Computers, Selected Papers*, second edition, Springer-Verlag, New York, 1975.

These are specially useful for details of the work of Mauchly, Eckert, Turing and von Neumann. Goldstine also contains a description of the evolution of differential analysers and the contribution of Bush.

A book which gives a summary of the history of computers, with Babbage getting pride of place and then includes articles on the state of computer development in 1953 is:
BOWDEN, B.V (editor) *Faster than Thought*, Pitman Publishing, London, 1953.

A fascinating and well-illustrated book is:
LAVINGTON, SIMON, *Early British Computers*, Manchester University Press, Manchester, 1980.

For details of certain specific machines, the following can be very useful, especially if coupled with a visit to the Science Museum, South Kensington:

SCIENCE MUSEUM, *Calculating Machines and Instruments* (D. Baxandall, revised by Jane Pugh), Science Museum, London 1975.

Biographies and histories of specific aspects of computing
Napier
GOLDSTINE, HERMAN H. *History of Numerical Analysis from the 16th through the 19th Century*, Springer-Verlag, New York, 1977.
This gives a sound, but interesting, mathematical description of the discovery and development of logarithms.

A rare but readable source book about Napier and logarithms is: KNOTT, C. G. (editor) *Napier Tercentenary Memorial Volume*, Longmans, Green and Co., London, 1915.

Pascal
MORTIMER, ERNEST, *Blaise Pascal*, Methuen, London, 1959.
This is a readable and informative biography.

Leibniz
HOFMANN, JOSEPH E. *Leibniz in Paris 1672–1676*, Cambridge University Press, Cambridge, 1974.
This is a scholarly and detailed account of Leibniz mathematical work. It does not give details of his calculating machine.

Babbage
MORRISON, PHILIP and EMILY (editors), *Charles Babbage and his Calculating Engines*, Dover Publications, Inc., New York, 1961.
This contains a readable biographical sketch and a selection of Babbage's own writings.

Bush
Some flavour of the use of differential analysers can be gleaned from: CRANK, J., *The Differential Analyser*, Longmans, Green and Co., London, 1947.

Turing
TURING, S., *Alan M. Turing*, W. Heffer and Sons, Cambridge, 1959.

A biography written by his mother.

Von Neumann

HEIMS, STEVE J., *John von Neumann and Norbert Wiener*, the MIT Press, Cambridge, Massachusetts, 1980.

A joint biography, not all of which is relevant to the development of the computer.

A readable first-hand account of some of his ideas is given in: VON NEUMANN, JOHN, *The Computer and the Brain*, Yale University Press, New Haven, Conn., 1958.

Index